More Advance Praise for *Building a House for Diversity*

"Roosevelt Thomas teaches all of us in corporate America a lesson about taking responsibility for valuing diversity in the workplace. His unique way of anecdotal storytelling calls on us to reaffirm our own personal commitment to diversity."
—Jim Wall, National Managing Director of
Human Resources, Deloitte & Touche

"Thomas makes a major contribution to managers at all levels who are struggling to manage the competing demands for business success: organization productivity and a work environment that honors diverse individual needs. His use of a metaphor of giraffes and elephants provides a meaningful context for the mix of case presentations and analyses, and self-assessment tools, which are useful and thought-provoking."
—Richard Beckhard, Professor of Management (Retired),
Sloan School of Management, MIT

"Thomas is truly a pioneer. Once again, he challenges the boundaries of our comfort zones in order to expand our understanding of diversity. In addition to breaking new philosophical ground, *Building a House for Diversity* provides concrete actions and specific behaviors that can transform committed individuals into mature diversity leaders. The book presents a complex subject in a lighthearted, easy-to-follow manner."
—Marcia L. Worthing, Executive Vice President,
Mullin & Associates/Lincolnshire International

"With today's significant demographic and sociologic changes, businesses are struggling with the transformation from employee uniformity (assimilation) to workforce unity. Thomas's simple but forceful fable of the elephant and giraffe, as illustrated in real-life case studies, provides not only encouragement but also applicable skills for our individual and corporate journey to become effective diversity respondents and achieve diversity maturity."
—Mike Warren, Chairman & CEO, Energen Corporation

Building a House for Diversity

How a Fable About a Giraffe & an Elephant
Offers New Strategies for Today's Workforce

R. Roosevelt Thomas, Jr.

With

Marjorie I. Woodruff

HarperCollins
Leadership

AN IMPRINT OF HarperCollins

Building a House for Diversity

Published by HarperCollins Leadership,
an imprint of HarperCollins Focus LLC.

Any internet addresses, phone numbers, or company or product information printed in this book are offered as a resource and are not intended in any way to be or to imply an endorsement by HarperCollins Leadership, nor does HarperCollins Leadership vouch for the existence, content, or services of these sites, phone numbers, companies, or products beyond the life of this book.

Bulk discounts available. For details visit:
www.harpercollinsleadership.com/bulkquotes
Email: customercare@harpercollins.com

ISBN 978-1-4002-3241-3 (TP)

To Ruby, my wife

Table of Contents

Foreword

A journalist reportedly once asked Albert Einstein why there had been so little progress in the social sciences compared to the enormous gains in the physical sciences. Einstein, we are told, responded by saying, "The social sciences are more difficult."

Throughout my career, this story continues to remind me that effective interpersonal skills are an absolute requirement for anyone who hopes to motivate people. It also serves notice that achieving these skills is never easy.

Identifying and managing the many facets of diversity are particularly interesting challenges, ones that Dr. Roosevelt Thomas, Jr., has been willing to meet head-on.

I first met Dr. Thomas when he spoke at a management seminar at Sunstrand Corporation, where I was CEO. In 1994, when I moved to McDonnell Douglas, I asked Dr. Thomas to speak to our top-management team. Both times, he engaged and inspired his listeners.

When McDonnell Douglas and Boeing merged, I had another opportunity to engage Dr. Thomas and his consulting and training group. This time my mission was broader. As a company, we wanted to embark on a program that would allow us to manage diversity in ways that would give us a competitive advantage. We asked Dr. Thomas and his firm to lead us on our journey. We aren't there yet, but we know what we don't know, and we've made some definite progress.

Building a House for Diversity can help you in your own personal diversity journey. It addresses the role we play in life and our personal responsibility for how we respond to diversity. The fable of the giraffe and the elephant is really a fable about everyday life. This fable, and the very human stories that follow, reflect experiences that people face throughout their careers. You will find yourself in this book, whether you are a "giraffe" or an "elephant."

Building a House for Diversity can awaken you and your team to the complexity and ambiguity of diversity issues. It reminds you that diversity is much more than race and gender, and it shows you how to manage diversity in a very practical way to support business goals. It also gives you the opportunity to ask yourself how well you have addressed diversity mixtures and tensions in the past and how prepared you are to address them in the future.

This book is imaginative in using a giraffe-and-elephant fable to introduce its major issues. It is practical in providing pre- and post-test diversity maturity indices to encourage self-assessment and case studies that illustrate the impact of your approach to diversity mixtures.

This last may be particularly important. Our approach and response to diversity affect tremendously our approach and response to change and novelty. As such, they ultimately influence our approach to life.

—Harry C. Stonecipher
President and COO
The Boeing Company

Preface

This book begins with a fable—a story about a giraffe and an elephant and their encounter with diversity. This fable, like others throughout the centuries, makes a point in a way that is both more vivid and appealing than a similar narrative about two people. Yet its lessons are applicable to people—more specifically, to people within organizations.

This applicability becomes clear in the chapters that follow. These chapters introduce you to eleven people who face diversity challenges on the job and have addressed them with varying degrees of success. These are real people. (Note that I have given them fictitious names and disguised their companies for this book.) With the exception of Phil Jackson, legendary coach of the Chicago Bulls, they were interviewed and asked to tell their stories, using their own words.

From each person and story, something valuable can be learned. Some of these people are intuitively adept at certain skills and not others; most are better at understanding one aspect than another; all are struggling to deal more effectively with the differences and similarities demonstrated by workforce participants in an increasingly diverse workplace. My hope is that the combined realities of their experiences demonstrate the organic learning process that ultimately leads to diversity effectiveness.

The book rests on the premise that individuals at all organizational levels are responsible for helping to create an organizational environment that works for all. It also rests on the belief that individuals who approach workforce diversity with confidence and address it with skill not only help their organizations to approach, address, and leverage diversity in ways that offer competitive advantage but enhance their personal career success as well.

Why is this so? The reason is that careers are much more likely to get bogged down because of an inability to work productively with others than because of a dearth of technical skills, and these others are increasingly likely to be different from ourselves. The reality of a diverse workforce means that organizations must create environments that allow all qualified employees to perform at peak effectiveness.

The approach in this book differs from most others. Most diversity efforts focus primarily on fostering managerial diversity competencies and pay relatively little attention to the mindsets and skills required of individuals at all organizational levels. In addition, they act as if individuals at all hierarchical levels experience diversity similarly. In fact, as the case studies indicate, they do not, and as a result, many initially successful diversity thrusts are compromised. Managers and individual contributors often understand the awareness message and are eager to work more harmoniously with those who are both similar to and different from themselves. But they still don't have a knowledge framework on which to base their actions or an understanding of the dynamics that accompany diversity. And they still need specific core skills that allow them to take timely and effective action around diversity-related issues.

Building a House for Diversity targets these issues. It can help individuals at all organizational levels learn to respond effectively to diversity—that is, to become what I call *effective diversity respondents*. By this, I mean people who act with confidence, wisdom, and effectiveness when interacting with others who may be significantly different from themselves in any number of ways. The confidence and wisdom come from what I call *diversity maturity*: a combination of knowledge—about diversity and its concepts and dynamics—and a comfort with these dynamics. The adeptness comes from mastery of core diversity management skills. The book can prove invaluable to managers who want to ratchet up their organization's progress with diversity management by developing individual diversity competencies as well.

One way it does this is to encourage both careful reading and active participation. The book contains a pre- and post-Personal Diversity Maturity Index. These allow you to assess your knowledge of and comfort with diversity principles and dynamics both before and after reading the book. Completing these self-assessments will encourage you to read the case studies with an eye out for similarities to your own situation and typical responses and will provide objective evidence of the progress with diversity maturity that you have made as a result of reading this book.

Finally, the book examines the link between organizational diversity maturity and personal diversity maturity, and offers guidelines for managers wishing to create a diversity-effective environment.

Building a House for Diversity complements the managerial and organizational prescriptions of my previous books, *Beyond Race and Gender: Unleashing the Power of Your Total Workforce by Managing Diversity* (AMACOM, 1991) and *Redefining Diversity* (AMACOM, 1996). It seeks to develop a framework that enables individual contributors to develop and improve their personal diversity competencies for use at work or in their personal lives. It is not necessary to have read these earlier books to understand or get the full benefit from this one. However, readers who want to broaden their understanding of organizational dynamics around diversity might want to consult them.

You can start now to learn how to become an effective diversity respondent by completing the pre-assessment version of the Personal Diversity Maturity Index.

Pre-Assessment

INSTRUCTIONS TO THE READER

Before you begin to read this book, take a moment to complete this Personal Diversity Maturity Index (PDMI) and assess your current "diversity maturity" level.

The PDMI is scenario-based. Please read each of the ten individual scenarios in its entirety and review the possible responses to each given situation. Then write the letter of the response that most closely reflects how you would respond to that scenario on the score sheet provided in Appendix B. When you have completed the pre-test PDMI, turn to your pre-test answer key in Appendix C for the scores applied to each response. Record your individual and aggregate scores on your score sheet. Turn to Appendix E for the interpretation of your aggregate score.

After reading the book, you will have another opportunity in Appendix F to complete a PDMI to compare your responses before and after reading the book. By completing the two different versions of the Index, you will have an opportunity to see how your diversity maturity has evolved as a result of reading the book.

1. *You manage a fast-food restaurant that had typically been staffed by younger people. Recently, you've added two older workers to the crew taking orders from customers. You're beginning to hear some mutterings from the younger staff about the older workers taking longer to prepare orders, chatting with customers, and being tentative about your computerized ordering system. What do you do?*

    a. Call a team meeting so that everyone can discuss what's going on at work and talk through their concerns.

    b. Ignore the problem. Your younger staff tend not to stay at the job for very long, so they'll soon be gone. The older staff will already be in place when newer young ones are hired, and these newer staff will simply take the older workers' way of doing business in stride.

    c. Assess the situation. Are the older workers doing a good job? Are their different work styles producing customer satisfaction or customer annoyance?

    d. Create teams of older and younger workers so that they can learn from each other. If that doesn't work out, reassign the older workers to jobs that aren't as time sensitive.

2. *You are active in a suburban, mostly white church that recently "adopted" an inner-city school that is 95 percent African American. You are responsible for working with twenty church members who will act as mentors to children at the school. All who have volunteered to be mentors are white. How would you address the situation?*

    a. Let matters rest. What's important is the commitment and personality of the individuals who will be mentors, not their skin color.

    b. Discuss the matter with African American members of your congregation to see what their thoughts are.

    c. Try to recruit more people of color to participate as mentors.

    d. Leave the need to better "match" mentors and students to other churches and community organizations.

3. *What is the most important reason to respond to diversity effectively?*

    a. It's the moral, right thing to do.

    b. It will make my company more competitive.

    c. The law requires it.

    d. It will help me get promoted.

4. *You are the local manager of a large chain hardware store, and you know that a competitor will soon open a new store nearby. The* *two stores are located in a middle-class, predominantly black neighborhood. You have three days to prepare a proposal for a special event designed to draw positive attention to your store. Which of the following best describes what you would do?*

a. You call your staff together to attend a meeting where you present the overall charge and hand out assignments. The staff forms into small groups and sends you daily reports. On day three, you pull the individual reports together into a package.

b. Given the short time frame, you decide that this is a responsibility you will handle yourself. You consult with your staff, but you handle all the details.

c. You recently worked with two people who really do razzle-dazzle stuff. There was a lot of creativity, which led to some tension and disagreement, but the results were terrific. You call those two people and give them the assignment.

d. You choose four employees who live in your store's community and are involved with organizations (churches, schools) in that community. You ask the four to help plan an event that will be responsive to the community's particular interests and priorities.

5. *You are the office manager of a large accounting firm that has a central pool of word processors and data entry personnel. One of your staff has very strong religious beliefs. A Bible is on his desk, and biblical pictures adorn his cubicle walls. During breaks, he often speaks to other staff about his church and encourages them to attend a service. Several of the staff have complained that they are having increasing difficulty remaining focused on their work. What would you do in this situation?*

a. Provide suggestions to the staff about how they might open a dialogue with this individual to explain their feelings.

b. Not do anything and hope things will settle down. You're concerned about infringing on his freedom of religion.

c. Talk with the employee. Explain that although he is

free to practice any religion of his choosing, his attempts to proselytize are interfering with the ability of others to do their job. Tell him he is free to keep the Bible and pictures where they are but that you expect him to refrain from discussing religion with others while in the work area.

d. Send out a memo to all staff stating that although your company welcomes differences in politics and religion, neither has any place in the office and should be confined to other activities they engage in.

6. *You belong to a ten-member technical group that meets weekly to go over progress and business developments. One member is an Asian American woman whose technical skills are superb and are valued by the group. However, the group has a strong preference for active verbal participation, and she tends to sit quietly during these meetings. How would you handle this situation?*

a. You recognize that there are probably some cultural factors at work here. But you also know that she's doing an excellent job. So you don't call the matter to your co-worker's or anyone else's attention.

b. You speak to your supervisor about your observations and ask her to encourage your co-worker to participate more in the meetings.

c. You seek out your co-worker and discuss your observations. You ask her if there's anything you can do to help her become more involved in these meetings.

d. During the meetings, you actively solicit input from your co-worker.

7. *You work in the research and development department of a manufacturing industry. Sales staff are always on your case, wanting to know when a "new, improved" product will be ready for market. They accuse the R&D folks of playing scientist and not realizing the importance of the company's bottom line. What do you do?*

a. Don't say anything. Salespeople will never understand R&D people, so there's no point in trying to get them to comprehend what you're trying to do.

    b. Acknowledge that the salespeople have some legitimate concerns, but let them know they don't fully understand the scientific development process.

    c. Establish a cross-functional group with representatives from R&D and sales. Set up lunch meetings for the purpose of problem solving around the issues and develop action plans that are compatible with the company's objectives.

    d. Look at your company's bottom line. Is sales making unreasonable demands that will adversely affect your company's ability to develop high-quality new products and stay competitive? Is R&D more interested in the beauty of scientific discovery than in your company's profitability? Base your decisions on your answers.

8. *Your firm, which had previously done business only in the United States, has recently expanded overseas. You've assigned a woman to head the team moving into a South American country. But word has come back that your major customer there is having a hard time accepting a woman heading up the effort. How do you respond?*

    a. Look into the situation further and determine whether it is her gender or some other factors (such as personality or skills) that are affecting the customer's views.

    b. Leave her in that position, but assign a man to be her special assistant and work with that customer.

    c. Replace her with a man because it is very important that your company demonstrate its commitment to customer needs.

    d. Contact the customer and ask what the company expects in the way of results from a team leader. Determine whether the current team leader can meet these expectations. If she can, tell the customer this and explain that you plan to keep her in the position. If she cannot meet expectations, assign the job to someone who can.

9. *Which of the following is likely to demonstrate the most diversity?*

    a. A conference attended by scientists of both genders and multiple ethnicities.

    b. A communitywide meeting for the purpose of determining how best to use a tax windfall.

    c. One white male, one African American male, one Hispanic male at a local sports event.

    d. I wouldn't know without observing and talking to the individuals present.

10. *You are a regional manager of a drugstore chain. You are getting ready to go into one of your stores when you hear two elderly women talking about a particular cashier. You introduce yourself to them and explain that, as a manager, you would like to know how their shopping experience was. One of the women explains that she felt very uncomfortable with the cashier who rang up her order. As the cashier was bagging the order, his shirtsleeve slid up and the woman noticed a tattoo on his forearm. She said, "I've been shopping here for years, and I always thought that you hired clean, presentable young people!" How should you respond to this customer?*

    a. Explain that your store prides itself on hiring quality employees who provide good service to customers, but also prides itself on letting employees express their individuality as long as it does not affect the service customers receive.

    b. Tell the customer you will talk to the cashier and ask him to cover the tattoo so that customers will not see it.

    c. Sympathize with the customer about "kids these days," but explain that the company's hands are tied—you can't interfere with an individual's right to express himself or you may get sued.

    d. Apologize for her experience and offer her a five-dollar coupon toward her next purchase at the store.

Acknowledgments

A number of individuals have contributed in a variety of ways to this book. I wish to acknowledge them.

I thank my wife, Ruby, and our children, Shane, April, and Jarred, for their continued support of "Dad's work." Their patience and understanding have allowed me to run with head giraffes, giraffes, and elephants as they address diversity. Their ongoing support has been of immeasurable value.

I also recognize the contributions of my mother, the late Icye P. Thomas, my grandmother, the late Lela M. Potts, and my father, Rufus R. Thomas, Sr. In their own unique ways, each encouraged me during my formative years.

I express gratitude to the head giraffes, giraffes, and elephants who shared their experiences for this book. However, I am also indebted to those who have permitted me to learn from them over the years and to develop with them. Without their support, I would not have been able to write this book.

My colleagues at R. Thomas Consulting and Training provided valuable help. Marjorie Woodruff, in addition to conducting some of the interviews, assisted me in refining the organization and clarity of my first draft. She also served as a sounding board as I identified and interpreted the interviews' lessons with respect to The Diversity Management Process. Thurmond Woodard and Elizabeth Holmes read the manuscript and offered helpful comments.

Once again, AMACOM's Adrienne Hickey, Executive Editor, gave professional and effective guidance as the project progressed.

I also acknowledge Maggie Stuckey's assistance in preparing the final draft of the manuscript. My executive assistant, Myke Harris-Long, managed the word-processing logistics.

Illustrations for this book were provided by Fentress & Associates. MACRO International developed the Personal Diversity Maturity Indices.

While I thank each individual and organization cited above for their contribution, I accept responsibility for this book. Hopefully, it will guide many head giraffes, giraffes, and elephants to the status of Effective Diversity Respondents.

PART ONE
A Modern Fable

1

The Giraffe and the Elephant

In a small suburban community just outside the city of Artiodact, a giraffe had a new home built to his family's specifications. It was a wonderful house for giraffes, with soaring ceilings and tall doorways. High windows ensured maximum light and good views while protecting the family's privacy. Narrow hallways saved valuable space without compromising convenience. So well done was the house that it won the National Giraffe Home of the Year Award. The home's owners were understandably proud.

One day the giraffe, working in his state-of-the-art wood shop in the basement, happened to look out the window. Coming down the street was an elephant. "I know him," he thought. "We worked together on a PTA committee. He's an excellent woodworker too. I think I'll ask him in to see my new shop. Maybe we can even work together on some projects." So the giraffe reached his head out the window and invited the elephant in.

The elephant was delighted; he had liked working with the giraffe and looked forward to knowing him better. Besides, he knew about the wood shop and wanted to see it. So he walked up to the basement door and waited for it to open.

"Come in; come in," the giraffe said. But immediately they encountered a problem. While the elephant could get his head in the door, he could go no farther.

"It's a good thing we made this door expandable to accommodate my wood shop equipment," the giraffe said. "Give me a minute while I take care of our problem." He removed some bolts and panels to allow the elephant in.

The two acquaintances were happily exchanging woodworking stories when the giraffe's wife leaned her head down the basement stairs and called to her husband: "Telephone, dear; it's your boss."

"I'd better take that upstairs in the den," the giraffe told the elephant. "Please make yourself at home; this may take a while."

The elephant looked around, saw a half-finished project on the lathe table in the far corner, and decided to explore it further. As he moved through the doorway that led to that area of the shop, however, he heard an ominous scrunch. He backed out, scratching his head. "Maybe I'll join the giraffe upstairs," he thought. But as he started up the stairs, he heard them begin to crack. He jumped off and fell back against the wall. It too began to crumble. As he sat there disheveled and dismayed, the giraffe came down the stairs.

"What on earth is happening here?" the giraffe asked in amazement.

"I was trying to make myself at home," the elephant said.

The giraffe looked around. "Okay, I see the problem. The doorway is too narrow. We'll have to make you smaller. There's an aerobics studio near here. If you'd take some classes there, we could get you down to size."

"Maybe," the elephant said, looking unconvinced.

"And the stairs are too weak to carry your weight," the giraffe continued. "If you'd go to ballet class at night, I'm sure we could get you light on your feet. I really hope you'll do it. I like having you here."

"Perhaps," the elephant said. "But to tell you the truth, I'm not sure that a house designed for a giraffe will ever really work for an elephant, not unless there are some major changes."

We've all heard the saying, "A picture is worth a thousand words." Experience tells me that a picture story may be twice as powerful. For years, I have used giraffe and elephant stories to help people understand the dynamics of diversity: what it really is, how it works, how we have traditionally dealt with it, and why our efforts have so often fallen short.

This particular story has much to teach us.

THE TRUE MEANING OF DIVERSITY

The elephant and the giraffe represent a diversity mixture, which I have defined as any combination of individuals who are different in some ways and similar in others. It is in this collective mixture that true diversity lives.

This is a critical concept that challenges us to abandon our accustomed ways of thinking about diversity: that in any situation, organization, or society there are the "main" people and then the "others"—those who are different in some way (usually race or gender). In this traditional view, it is the "others" who constitute the diversity.

Once we begin to see diversity as the total collective mixture, made up of the "main" ones and also the "others," it becomes obvious that diversity is not a function of race or gender or any other us-versus-them dyad, but a complex and ever-changing blend of attributes, behaviors, and talents.

The giraffe and elephant form a diversity mixture of animals. They are similar in important ways: they live in the same neighborhood, share several interests (woodworking, PTA involvement), and have a congenial attitude toward each other and a desire to become better friends. But they are also different in several critical ways—size, weight, and shape—and those differences prove to be their undoing.

In our story, the giraffe represents the "main" group; it is his house, his design, his rules. He's in charge. The elephant is the "other." He is warmly invited and genuinely welcome, but in the giraffe's home he is the outsider and always will be. The house was not built with elephants in mind.

TRADITIONAL APPROACHES TO DIVERSITY

The experiences of the giraffe and the elephant also illustrate the essence of the three usual ways business organizations have chosen to deal with diversity: affirmative action, understanding differences, and diversity management.

When the giraffe decides to invite the elephant to visit, he makes a special effort to help him in by removing a panel to widen the door. This is *affirmative action*, which focuses on inclusion and calls for special action to correct imbalances.

The giraffe and elephant get along well. The giraffe invites the elephant in because he enjoys his company and wants to know him better. The elephant accepts the invitation for the same reasons. This is *understanding differences*, which focuses on relationships—how people in organizations get along.

When the visit proves disastrous, the giraffe proposes several corrective actions that the elephant should take. The elephant, however, resists bearing the full burden of making the necessary changes. He thinks that maybe they should also modify the giraffe's house. This two-way perspective is *diversity management*, which seeks to create an environment that accesses the talent of all participants.

DIVERSITY IN ACTION: KEY DYNAMICS

When we look closely at what happened during this brief and messy visit, we find that the giraffe and elephant have other important lessons to teach us about diversity.

◄ *Different components of a diversity mixture have different perspectives.* The giraffe and the elephant see the situation through different lenses. The giraffe is horrified by the destruction the elephant has created, and his automatic response is that the elephant must change, must abandon the qualities that make him an elephant and instead become more like a giraffe. He says, in effect, "Since you don't fit in my house, let's fix you."

The elephant isn't so sure. He knows he will remain an elephant, no matter how much he exercises or how well he dances. He also knows that a house built for a giraffe will never be comfortable for him, no matter how well he and its owner get along.

Unless the giraffe and elephant come up with more creative

solutions, their friendship is unlikely to survive. Their diversity exceeds their diversity management skills.

🪶 *Many are reluctant to embrace genuine diversity fully.* It is not an accident that the giraffe hopes to "fix" the elephant. He likes his house the way it is. Modifying this comfortable, award-winning structure has probably never entered his mind. It will take a compelling reason to convince him to do so. He may decide to relinquish his relationship with the elephant instead.

🪶 *Diversity tension is inevitable.* Wherever different perspectives are found, tension will exist. It is not a question of one party or the other's being at fault. It is not the same thing as conflict, and it is not invariably negative, but it is invariably present.

Both the giraffe and elephant are horrified by the damage that the elephant caused and distressed by the damage this has done to their budding friendship. What makes their distress more acute is that both were caught by surprise: they never anticipated that bringing the elephant into a giraffe house would cause problems. However, even if a joint team of giraffe and elephant architects were to build the perfect giraffe-elephant house, the two would still experience tension as they moved past surface topics and became more genuine with each other. Their task then would be to persevere in their efforts at friendship in the midst of this ongoing tension.

🪶 *Complexity inevitably accompanies diversity.* Both creatures are now faced with a complex situation. The giraffe is thinking, "My family and I could have lived here forever without making such a mess. How am I going to repair it, and who is responsible for paying?" The elephant wonders, "How did an innocent visit end up with a disaster like this?" Nevertheless, both give evidence that they understand that something worthwhile is at stake. They share a common interest in building a friendship. To reject diversity because it creates tension and complexity is to make a decision not to grow and flourish.

GIRAFFES AND ELEPHANTS: WHOSE HOUSE IS IT?

In the chapters that follow, I will be using elephants and giraffes as metaphors for humans, especially humans at work, where all the dynamics of diversity spring from the mixture of two types of people: those in the dominant group and those in a subordinate position. Dominance can be but isn't necessarily linked to a numerical majority. For example, whites were in the numerical minority in South Africa, yet they controlled the country for a long time. Similarly, women are in the numerical majority in many organizations but often placed in subordinate roles.

Members of the dominant component—the giraffes—are the people in control. They, or their ancestors, built the house. They decide the policies and procedures, set up the underlying assumptions for success, and establish systems to reflect those assumptions. Giraffes know the unwritten rules for success because they created them. They know how to play the game so they will win. They have a major voice in who is allowed to enter the organization and whether they will succeed or merely be tolerated.

Subordinate component members—the elephants—have little or no power. They are the newcomers, the outsiders. They lack insider knowledge, yet they must somehow figure out the unwritten rules for success and make the necessary adaptations. Their own intrinsic needs are not incorporated into the organization's environment, and in fact they feel pressure to ignore them or set them aside. To get along in someone else's house, they must leave their needs and their differences at the front door.

WHOSE JOB IS IT?

In the past, most of us concluded that dealing with something as complicated as diversity should be left to the managers and owners. We kept quiet about our own feelings, waiting for the bosses to figure out the company's official position.

We were wrong. Diversity is not simply a management "problem" that "they" should handle. It is a fact of modern organizational life, and everyone in the company, top to bottom, contributes to it. If genuine diversity is to thrive in organizations, it will be because the right climate has been created. And that climate is the product of the beliefs and behaviors of all workforce participants: managers and nonmanagers, dominant group and subordinate group members.

Nurturing such a climate depends not on how one group or the other perceives diversity. It depends instead on the mind-sets and actions of individual members of both groups and on the way they interact with each other.

This is the final thing the elephant and giraffe can teach us: *True diversity management begins and ends with individuals.* It begins with each of us accepting our responsibility as actors in the diversity scenario, and it ends with our acquiring certain specific skills and achieving a level of maturity in our thinking and acting about diversity.

The giraffe and the elephant have not yet reached this place. The giraffe does not accept personal responsibility for diversity, and neither the giraffe nor the elephant has much experience in the skills of diversity management. Thus, by letting us see what they lack and the disastrous consequences of that lack, they have given us the most important lesson of all.

🦒 2 🐘
Diversity Effectiveness: An Overview

This chapter sets out the interlocking ideas, dynamics, and skills that combine to form the ideal state of diversity effectiveness. They are separated into individual components and presented one at a time in linear sequence, because there is no other way to construct a book.

But real life is seldom so tidy. In organizational settings where diversity is an issue, the ideas presented here as stand-alone concepts are in fact as complex and interlinked as pieces in a kaleidoscope. All the pieces are connected to all the other pieces and to the whole. They interact with one another, and in that interaction change the reality. Make one small twist on the kaleidoscope, and the pieces shift into another pattern.

This chapter, then, is something of a preview. All the fundamental principles of diversity effectiveness are unfurled here, in abbreviated fashion, so that you will begin to become familiar with the concepts and the terminology. As you read more about them in the chapters that follow, you will already have an understanding of where each fits into the larger picture. The notations here link you directly to those later chapters, where you can observe abstract ideas taking tangible shape in the sometimes messy reality of actual situations.

THE EFFECTIVE DIVERSITY RESPONDENT

The giraffe and the elephant are not unique in their predicament. In companies large and small, people at all hierarchical levels struggle with diversity issues and with their role in resolving them. They engage in the struggle, even though it is occasionally uncomfortable, because they want to respond to diversity consistently in ways that help to achieve their personal goals and also their organization's objectives. In doing so, they are becoming what I call *effective diversity respondents* (EDRs), people who demonstrate an organic blend of diversity maturity and core diversity skills.

The word *maturity* evokes thoughts of good judgment and wisdom that flow from experience. Mature professionals command respect because their performance draws on experience as well as technical or professional expertise. Diversity maturity signifies a deep clarity about the fundamental concepts of diversity and a certain sophistication in thinking and understanding, We can acquire the conceptual clarity and learn the diversity principles through education (formal and informal) and personal reflection. Maturity comes with putting these principles into action on a daily basis.

The diversity skills can be learned as well, for they are relatively straightforward. But mastering them takes practice. Furthermore, the skills by themselves, even when adequately mastered, are not sufficient to bring about genuine diversity effectiveness. To assume that they are is the equivalent of assuming a fifteen-year-old who can steer the car and hit the brake pedal is a competent driver.

Diversity effectiveness, like driving expertise, requires both maturity and skills. Neither is acquired quickly or painlessly. Fortunately, developing a mature mind-set and practicing the skills work to reinforce each other: while practicing the skills, we gain maturity; with increased maturity, we find the skills have become easier.

Diversity Maturity

Diversity-mature individuals regularly do the following:

- Accept personal responsibility for enhancing their own and their organization's effectiveness.
- Demonstrate contextual knowledge. That is, they know themselves and their organizations, and they understand key diversity concepts and definitions.

    ◀   Are clear about requirements and base include/exclude
decisions about differences on how they impact the ability to meet these requirements.

    ◀   Understand that diversity is accompanied by complexity
and tension and are prepared to cope with these in pursuit of greater diversity effectiveness.

    ◀   Are willing to challenge conventional wisdom.

    ◀   Engage in continuous learning.

Accept Responsibility

Diversity-mature individuals see themselves, not others, as
responsible for addressing diversity effectively. They understand
the impact of organizational culture on diversity-related practices,
but they don't use it as an excuse for inaction or indifference.

They say, in effect, "I am an actor. I cannot blame my lack of
diversity effectiveness on my upbringing, my boss, the training
department, or any other part of the organization. Only one person is responsible for how I relate to diversity now: me. And only
one person has the power to make changes in this area: me."

One immediate outcome of this way of thinking is to put
yourself into the diversity mix— to see yourself as being as different and similar as others. This is not as simple as it sounds. It is
very tempting to think of diversity as "all those others"; but taking
responsibility for your own role in diversity effectiveness means
placing yourself squarely in the mix, along with everyone else.

To see what self-responsibility looks like, read about the experiences of Phil Jackson (Chapter 3), Bill Smith (Chapter 4),
Joan (Chapter 8), and Kirk (Chapter 12). Debra (Chapter 7) alter-
nates in her ability to accept responsibility for her role in the
mix, and Ray (Chapter 6) prefers not to acknowledge that there
is a mix.

Demonstrate Contextual Knowledge

Individuals who know themselves and their organizations,
understand diversity concepts, and act on this knowledge and
understanding demonstrate contextual knowledge.

An Understanding of Self. People who are engaged in the process of working toward diversity effectiveness know that the journey begins with themselves. They develop personal goals, objectives, and requirements and review them periodically. They also stay mindful of whether the setting they are in meets, or is capable of meeting, their significant personal requirements.

Several of the people you will meet in the coming chapters demonstrate this search for self-knowledge: Joan, Richard (both in Chapter 8), Jeff (Chapter 11), and Kirk (Chapter 12). This idea is discussed in more detail in Chapters 9 and 13 as well.

Diversity-mature people also assess what they believe and feel about diversity, for they understand that in modern business organizations, their level of diversity effectiveness can play an important role in achieving their personal goals.

As you read the stories of Phil Jackson and Richard (Chapters 3 and 8, respectively), you will observe two men who have given a great deal of thought to this issue.

Readers aiming for greater diversity effectiveness would do well to ask themselves the personal diversity questions.

PERSONAL DIVERSITY QUESTIONS

- Am I comfortable working with people from all demographic groups?
- Is there a group or groups that I struggle to accept?
- If so, how have I attempted to overcome my biases?
- How will my comfort or lack of comfort with people different from me affect my ability to advance within this workplace?
- Do I enjoy diversity?
- If so, what kind?
- If so, how much?

An Understanding of the Organization. Diversity-mature individuals understand their organization as well as themselves. They know that by helping their organization achieve its objectives, they make progress in achieving their personal goals.

Mission and Vision. Diversity-mature individuals understand why it is vital to analyze their organization and learn the answers to these questions:

◀ What is the company's vision?
◀ Its mission?
◀ Its principal objectives?
◀ Its key strategies?

Understanding the company's mission and vision is, of course, important for all employees who wish to make a significant contribution. But here we are speaking specifically about these issues in relation to diversity. Clearly articulating the mission leads directly to articulating the business motive for diversity.

The Business Motive. Organizations increasingly understand that managing diversity well is a business necessity that benefits them in both the workplace and the marketplace. Diversity leaders put the question this way: How does diversity effectiveness help us achieve our aspirations? If everyone in the company were to become skilled in responding to diversity, would that make a difference?

In addition to this big-picture understanding, diversity-mature people can identify which diversity mix or mixes are likely to have the most impact on the ability to achieve the mission and vision. This allows them to decide which mixes must be addressed, and why, and how.

In both cases—the broad picture and the specific situation—asking the organizational diversity questions is a good way to achieve clarity.

Clarity about the business motive is discussed in Chapters 5, 9, and 13, the analysis chapters. It is demonstrated in the personal histories of Phil Jackson (Chapter 3) and Bill Smith (Chapter 4),who appear always to have kept the business motive firmly in mind. Joan (Chapter 8) and Kirk (Chapter 12) appear to do this as well. Jeff (Chapter 11) does not have this understanding.

ORGANIZATIONAL DIVERSITY QUESTIONS

- Do we need diversity in this organization (or in this situation)?
- If so, what kind?
- If so, how much?

Conceptual Clarity About Diversity. Effective diversity respondents have moved beyond equating "diversity" with differences in race and gender. They define *diversity* instead as any significant collective mixture that contains similarities as well as differences.

The elephant and the giraffe, whose story you read in Chapter 1, demonstrate this definition of genuine diversity. Joan's definition of diversity as a "multiplicity of thoughts and opinions and viewpoints" is relevant as well, as is Richard's broad-based understanding. (Both can be found in Chapter 8.) Kirk's (Chapter 12) recognition that "people have a bigger problem getting over beliefs and morals than they do getting over skin color" demonstrates this too.

An important part of this idea, and one that is often overlooked, is that diversity incorporates similarities as well as differences. Dealing with differences can take so much energy that we forget to acknowledge the similarities. Yet it is important not to do so. Effective diversity respondents know that awareness of similarities encourages cooperation and cohesion. In fact, the more complex the organization and situation are, the more important it is to have some commonality. Effective diversity respondents also know, however, that they must acknowledge and address differences as well. Overemphasis on similarities can mute diversity, thus dampening creativity and vitality in pursuit of an illusionary sameness. Achieving a balance may be most difficult for elephants, who must assess the rewards of uniqueness against those of assimilation. To a greater or lesser extent, the elephants in Part Three have all found this to be an important challenge.

Diversity-mature individuals know that diversity is not the same as inclusion. Achieving diversity is not the same as ensuring that the mixture reflects the total population of potential members. The first is about openness to differences in attitudes, perceptions, and behaviors. The second is more correctly termed *inclusion* and is an exercise in arithmetic: "Let's make sure we have some representatives from all categories, in some kind of proportion." Up to now, most companies have understood workforce diversity this way and have used affirmative action programs as their usual means of achieving it.

Diversity-mature individuals know that representation per se does not guarantee true diversity. This is an essential understanding. To say "diversity" and mean "representation" confuses the issues and hampers the ability to become truly effective at addressing diversity.

The distinction between diversity and inclusion may be seen most clearly by comparing the experiences of Phil Jackson (Chapter 3), who accepted Dennis Rodman's untraditional behaviors in an effort to access his talent, with those of Carol (Chapter 6), George (Chapter 10), and Jeff (Chapter 11). Each of the latter says "diversity" but means "inclusion." Indeed, most of the stories demonstrate some degree of confusion between diversity and inclusion. As you read, look for the connection between the level of confusion and the reduction in organizational effectiveness.

Diversity-mature people identify two major kinds of diversity: *attribute diversity* (such as ethnic group, age, and education) and *behavior diversity* (how people act in a certain situation, which may or may not be a function of some attribute). They know that we cannot judge a group's behavioral diversity by assessing its attribute diversity.

Within organizations, there are two key reasons for this. The first has to do with people. There is as much attitudinal, perceptual, and behavioral diversity within demographic groups as among them. The second has to do with the culture of the organization. In organizations where assimilation is the norm, there is unlikely to be much behavioral diversity regardless of who is in the room. In organizations where differences are accepted, a room full of white men may contain significant behavioral diversity. To confuse the two kinds of diversity and act on this confusion is to be less effective in addressing diversity than you would otherwise be.

This concept is described more fully in Chapter 13. You will see it in action most clearly in Chapter 7 (Mark and Debra) and Chapter 12 (Kirk), although most of the stories contain evidence of some confusion.

Are Clear About Requirements

Achieving the company's mission and vision through diversity management requires being able to distinguish between a genuine requirement and a preference, convenience, or tradition, and then basing actions on requirements, and nothing else. It sounds simple, but it is a common and serious stumbling block. Often a decision to accept or reject a certain element of a diversity mixture is rationalized with, "This is something we need," when in fact the truth is closer to, "I like it better this way," or "I don't agree with this behavior." Effective diversity respondents can identify the genuine requirements and consistently use them as a basis for making decisions about diversity.

Learning to distinguish real requirements is discussed in more detail in Chapters 5, 9, and 13. Those who have already learned this lesson include Phil Jackson (Chapter 3), Bill Smith (Chapter 4), Joan (Chapter 8), and Kirk (Chapter 12). Those who found this to be a stumbling block include Mark and Debra (Chapter 7) and Richard (Chapter 8). As you read, look for the link between acting on preferences, and personal frustration and reduced organizational effectiveness.

Cope With Diversity Complexity and Tension

Genuine diversity increases complexity. To choose one is to get the other. Diversity-mature individuals don't shrink from this complexity; they accept it as part of the diversity package.

The elephant and the giraffe, as we read in Chapter 1, encountered complexity, to their mutual dismay. Humans who understand and accept complexity include Phil Jackson (Chapter 3), Bill Smith (Chapter 4), Richard (Chapter 8), and Kirk (Chapter 12). Ray (Chapter 6), Mark (Chapter 7), George (Chapter 10), and Jeff (Chapter 11) struggle with it.

Diversity-mature individuals know that when people with different backgrounds, perspectives, and objectives express themselves openly, there will be tension. This tension is not inherently positive or negative, good or bad; it simply is. Tension that promotes healthy competition can be good. Tension that immobilizes a unit is clearly not.

The difficulty is that many individuals, like many organizations, are so uncomfortable with tension that they focus on eliminating it rather than managing it. They place more importance on harmony than on achieving objectives.

Diversity-mature individuals learn to function in the face of tension. They know it isn't personal but rather is part and parcel of the dynamics of diversity.

Phil Jackson (Chapter 3) shows great skill in putting tension in perspective and managing it well, as do Bill Smith (Chapter 4) and Richard (Chapter 8). Kirk (Chapter 12) also handles it well. Ray and Carol (both in Chapter 6), Debra (Chapter 7), and George (Chapter 10) are clearly uncomfortable with it.

However, tension and conflict are not the same. Tension becomes conflict when it is responded to ineptly. Diversity conflict arises when people ask unproductive questions, such as, "What's wrong with you that you aren't more like me?"

Are Willing to Challenge Conventional Wisdom

Diversity-mature individuals have challenged conventional wisdom and made mind-set shifts along the way.

Place Differences in Context

Recently some organizations, to encourage the acceptance and valuing of all employees, have focused on "celebrating differences," the implication being that all differences are good.

Effective diversity respondents, however, know that differences simply are. They exist. Whether they are good, bad, or neutral depends on the context: that is, whether the difference has any effect, either positive or negative, on the organization's ability to accomplish its goals. Effective diversity respondents base "accept" or "reject" decisions on how the differences mesh with these realities. They can accept attributes that fit even when their personal preferences are violated.

The importance of evaluating differences in context is given further attention in the personal stories of Phil Jackson (Chapter 3), Bill Smith (Chapter 4), Carol (Chapter 6), Richard (Chapter 8), and Kirk (Chapter 12).

Let Go of Hindering Concepts. Diversity-mature individuals are able to let go of hindering concepts; that is, they can do key "unlearning." They need to reject, if they have not already done so, the notion that only those with exceptional interpersonal skills can succeed with diversity management.

These individuals don't discount the need to challenge stereotypes, be open to differences, or be flexible, all commonly cited as necessary "characteristics" from which to approach diversity. But they don't see these as personality traits or characteristics, which are either innate or require special training to achieve. They know that individuals willing to learn the diversity concepts and make the mind-set shifts will find that the process elicits from them the necessary behaviors.

Joan (Chapter 8) and Kirk (Chapter 12) have learned that effective diversity skills don't depend on inherent traits.

Engage in Continuous Learning

Diversity-mature individuals know that they are engaged in a continuous learning process. Diversity effectiveness requires a willingness and ability to monitor both yourself and the environment, to challenge yourself regularly, and to devise specific ways to work with the new concepts so that eventually they become second nature.

The benefits of continuous learning and the costs of its absence are demonstrated explicitly or implicitly in each of the stories in the following chapters.

Effective diversity respondents have worked to acquire contextual knowledge, an understanding of diversity and its major concepts, and a comfort with diversity's dynamics. But to put these principles into action consistently, they need one thing more: a framework process. Such a process, once internalized, provides a structure for deciding how to act in specific situations. It helps people size up a situation quickly and address it effectively and efficiently. It serves as a guide to determining what they should be doing and monitoring how well they are doing it.

My earlier work, *Redefining Diversity*,[1] offers such a framework. It consists of three steps, which we can also think of as three core diversity skills: The consistent use of the process together with the skills embedded within it is the second of the two requirements for becoming an effective diversity respondent.

Core Diversity Skills: A Framework Process

◀ *Ability to identify diversity mixtures and their related tensions.* Since unidentified mixtures can't be addressed, this is a critical skill. On the surface it seems simple and straightforward, yet many fail to master it. There is a natural tendency to focus on the diversity mixtures in which they have an interest, and to ignore others.

In several of the stories that follow, people overemphasize one diversity dimension—usually race or gender—at the expense of identifying other mixtures that may be having more effect on whether they achieve their goals.

◀ *Ability to analyze the mixtures and related tensions.* Not all identified mixtures need be addressed—only those that interfere with achieving goals. How key is the mixture? How disruptive are the tensions? Is any action needed? Will taking action help meet significant organizational objectives?

Phil Jackson (Chapter 3) and Bill Smith (Chapter 4) demonstrate an ability to make such an analysis. In several of the stories, the same overemphasis on a "pet" diversity dimension that led to a failure to identify significant mixtures discourages people from determining which mixtures and tensions are in most need of being addressed.

◀ *Ability to select an appropriate response.* If action is needed, what should that action be? A framework process helps by presenting a consistent structure for evaluating possible actions. The process described in *Redefining Diversity* outlines eight generic action options that may apply in any given situation. (These eight options include (1) increase/decrease, (2) deny, (3) assimilate, (4) suppress, (5) isolate, (6) tolerate, (7) build future relationships, and (8) foster mutual adaptation. They are described in the appendix of this book.) They serve as a kind of mental checklist to guide people through a chain of thinking that ensures they will have the greatest number of options to consider. The skill lies in being able to sort quickly through the possible options and choose the most effective one. Like most other skills, it is best learned through practice.[2]

Adeptness with these three critical skills is analyzed in all of the interview chapters. Those with the most commitment to inclusion and assimilation are least likely to demonstrate these skills. Those most comfortable with behavior diversity are most likely to employ them. The consistent use of the process together with the skills embedded within it is the second of the two requirements for becoming an effective diversity respondent.

Effective diversity respondents demonstrate a kind of diversity maturity that allows them to internalize key diversity concepts and use them to inform their actions. They are adept at applying the core diversity skills as well. Both diversity maturity and demonstration of the core skills require education, training, and practice. The result—becoming an effective diversity respondent—is worth the effort.

NOTES

1. Thomas, R. Roosevelt, Jr., *Redefining Diversity* (New York: AMACOM, 1996).
2. Ibid.

MR. GIRAFFE

PART TWO
Head Giraffes in Action

If giraffes are the people who own the house, head giraffes are the people who are ultimately in charge. It is they who decide where the organization will go and how it will get there. And it is they who determine the culture that exists inside the house.

The attitudes, beliefs, and practices of chief executive officers—head giraffes of organizations—have an enormous impact on what happens and how within their organizational house. Theirs is an all-encompassing charge.

In the next two chapters you will meet two head giraffes. One was until recently the head of a major sports organization; the other is the president of a subsidiary unit of a major industrial company. Both demonstrate an extraordinary level of skill and maturity in dealing with diversity.

🦒 3 🦒
A Natural Diversity Manager: Phil Jackson

Phil Jackson/Chicago Bulls

Basketball fans watching the World Championship Chicago Bulls romp their way to another victory didn't turn to each other and say, "That Phil Jackson is a great diversity manager."

Yet if managing diversity is about pursuing collective objectives with individuals who are qualified but significantly different, Jackson is a diversity manager extraordinaire. He led his team of headstrong, disparate, talented, and aging players to seven National Basketball Association (NBA) championships in nine years.

Jackson's success was no accident. It was instead the result of a clearly defined mission and vision, a unified philosophy, a strategic model, and effective techniques used in the service of identified requirements. During his phenomenal years with the Bulls, Jackson was able to create a basketball "house" that worked for an enormously gifted and diverse group of elephants and giraffes, and for himself as head giraffe.

Creating a Team

In 1988 Phil Jackson assumed the role of the Bulls' coach with a dream of winning championships in a way that combined his two greatest passions: basketball and spiritual exploration (defined as examining the relationship between the inner and outer life).

His goal was to build a team that would "blend individual talent with a heightened group consciousness—a team that could win big without becoming small in the process."[1]

Clearly Jackson had his work cut out for him. His first challenge was to make a team out of a group of disparate and disaffected individuals, dominated by the immensely talented and frustrated Michael Jordan. Jordan, a global phenomenon, a "Michelangelo in baggy shorts," had scored an average of thirty-five points in the 1987–1988 season, winning his first of several scoring titles.[2] But the team itself had not had a winning season, and this had left Jordan an angry man and alienated him from his teammates.

Jackson's Approach

No ordinary methods would do in creating the team Jackson envisioned. He approached the challenge from a spiritual, practical, and symbolic perspective. His aim was to create a team environment founded in the concept of selflessness he had built from personal involvement with Christianity, Zen Buddhism, and the teachings of the Lakota Sioux.[3] He believed that such an environment would facilitate the sense of connectedness that he saw as key to the team's success.

Clearly, the team he had committed to coach lacked any such sense of connectedness. If he was to build it, Jackson would have to empower the players who shared the court with Jordan. For this he needed more than a philosophy; he also needed a broadly based strategy and a compelling metaphor.

The Triangle Offense

Jackson found his strategy in the "triangle offense of Tex Winter," his former coach and mentor. This offense, described by some as a "five-man tai chi," emphasizes cooperation and freedom. It orchestrates the flow of movement and lures the defense off balance. It also empowers individual players while requiring that they remain attentive to the group.[4]

To Jackson, this dual capacity to make individual and collective decisions throughout the game was key. He believed that once players had mastered the system, their group intelligence would exceed that of the coach or any one player.

The person least likely to be enthusiastic about the system was the one who had the most to lose, the one who was already making the most visible contribution to the team. If the team offense were to succeed, Michael Jordan would have to agree to the possibility of scoring less and risking his scoring championships by sharing the offense with players in whom he had demonstrated very little confidence.

Jordan struggled. In principle, he was receptive to the triangle concept. But its implementation could cost him points. He alternated between cooperation and rebellion, raising the possibility that the offense would not stick. Jackson remained sanguine, confident that Michael and his newly empowered—and challenged—teammates would adjust, and the strategy would succeed. He was right.

The Sacred Journey Metaphor

The success of the triangle strategy ensured that the players would work as a team. However, it could not facilitate the spiritual exploration that Jackson saw as essential. This, he believed, required an overarching metaphor and the learning of spiritually based concepts and techniques.

For Jackson, who had attended basketball clinics at the Pine Ridge Reservation, home of the Lakota Sioux, the choice of a metaphor was easy. It was the Lakota warrior and his ``sacred journey.''[5]

Lakota warriors saw everything, even their enemies, as sacred, and all of life as interconnected. Their tribal unity was based on this interconnectedness. A warrior sought not to stand out from his fellow band members, but rather to act bravely and honorably to help the group however possible.

Jackson had concluded that the Bulls defeated themselves when playing against the Detroit Pistons by letting their anger disrupt their concentration. He sought a blueprint that would help players to keep their minds clear, unclouded by anger. Such a blueprint, he believed, could be found in the Lakotas' approach, which honored the humanity of both sides while recognizing that only one victor could emerge.[6]

To make these ideals concrete, Jackson decorated the Bulls' team room with Native American totems and other symbolic objects. He wanted to create an environment where the "spirit of the team" would take form.[7]

Mental Discipline

Jackson knew that his team needed one more skill to complement the team-building offensive strategy and the overarching spiritual paradigm: mental discipline. This he found in Zen Buddhism.

Jackson's interest in Buddhist ideas began as the result of a baseball injury during his freshman year at college. His brother suggested self-hypnosis to help get his pitching rhythm back, and introduced him to the Zen concept of mindfulness, a meditation practice. Its goal is an uncluttered mind that allows maximum awareness of and participation in the moment.[8]

Jackson saw the value of this concept for his team. Basketball, he notes, "is a complex dance that requires shifting from one objective to another at lightning speed. To excel, you need to act with a clear mind and be totally focused on what everyone on the floor is doing at that very moment."[9]

To help his players pursue the ideal of an uncluttered mind, Jackson also introduced visualization. Then he added one more Buddhist idea, a philosophy that lends a liberating perspective to winning and losing. "Things are more likely to go your way when you stop worrying about whether you're going to win or lose and focus your full attention on what's happening *right this moment*," he said.[10]

Acquisition of Dennis Rodman

The 1995 acquisition of Dennis Rodman, like the earlier "Jordan problem," put Jackson's concepts and practices to the test. Predictions were rife that Rodman would compromise Jackson, the Bulls, and their model. "Here's the short list of who would be better news than Dennis Rodman for the Bulls: Typhoid Mary, Moammar Gadhafi, Charles Manson, Lizzie Borden, Jeffrey Dahmer," wrote one sports writer.[11]

But Jackson was willing to take the risk. Horace Grant's retirement had cost the Bulls their rebounding capability, and Jordan's return from baseball resulted in a difficult adjustment for him and the team. The Bulls had been eliminated in the second round of the 1994–1995 NBA playoffs. Jackson was looking in earnest for a power player who could rebound.

Dennis Rodman could do that. He was a strong rebounder who enjoyed a reputation as a quality player who played hard, did basketball's dirty work (defense, rebounding, and scrapping for loose balls), and didn't worry about fitting in.[12]

Yet Rodman came with liabilities: a history of suspensions for missing practices and leaving games and for refusing to join the huddle during the championship playoff series; a series of absences for a dislocated shoulder; and a fondness for outrageous behavior, including nontraditional dress and frequent hair color changes.[13] Rodman had one other liability: He was the antithesis of the type of player the Bulls' director of personnel preferred.

Still, the requirement for a talented rebounder convinced the Bulls to talk to him. After talking to Rodman about the incidents from his past, as well as his ability to fit in with triangle offense, Jackson decided to take a chance. With the acquiescence of the personnel director and the agreement of co-captains Jordan and Scottie Pippen, he offered Rodman a place on the team.[14]

All did not go smoothly. There were suspensions, missed games, resentments, and contract disputes. But Rodman, who promised Jackson an NBA championship, did his part to make it happen, and Jackson gave Rodman leeway to be himself. Jackson also proved himself a master of matching rewards to requirements, placing incentives in Rodman's 1997–1998 contract. As a result, Rodman played consistently and earned more than he had before.

In 1998, the Bulls won their third consecutive championship. Clearly, Jackson had led his team of powerful and diverse players in a way that maximized their abilities both as individuals and as a team.

At the end of the 1998 season, Jackson announced that he was stepping down as the Bulls' coach. He did not announce his future plans. Few doubt, however, that he will find a different arena in which to display his unique management skills.

JACKSON AS EFFECTIVE DIVERSITY RESPONDENT

When Jackson joined the Bulls as assistant coach, he found a winning, entertaining, and underachieving team. This group of players differed in talent, level of development, years with the team, celebrity status, personality, and degree of satisfaction with the team as well.

His task was to endow players with a unity of purpose and a commitment to the team, and to empower them to perform at their best in the service of this team. His greatest obstacle to achieving these goals was the skewedness of the team, which had been thrown off balance by the "Jordan problem." The diversity of the team was, in short, both his greatest challenge and his greatest opportunity.

Basketball as Sacred Journey

The most far-reaching manifestation of Jackson's creative intertwining of disparate elements in pursuit of a larger whole is his combining of basketball and spiritual exploration to create a mission and vision for the Bulls. The Bulls were to be an empowered and inclusive team—one whose members played in the moment and responded to each other with compassion and respect. The quest for the NBA championship was to be a sacred journey.[15]

Creating a Culture to Support a Dream

Jackson came to the task uniquely prepared by experience, training, personal history, and predisposition. He set out to sculpt a mission and vision for his team, creatively combining Lakota philosophy and symbols with Zen Buddhist practices, with their shared focus on interconnectedness. A basketball team with a spiritual base? As far-fetched as it may have seemed at first, that spiritual exploration allowed Jackson to create a unique model of success: a team composed of empowered players who played in the moment and responded to each other with compassion and respect, undertaking the quest for the NBA championship as a sacred journey.

To support this vision and reaffirm his model, Jackson began to build an organizational culture based on five fundamental assumptions:

1. If we can place the game of basketball within the context of spirituality, we can make a greater commitment, experience deeper satisfaction, and win—although winning is not everything.
2. If we play as a team, we can win.
3. If we play with compassion, we can win.
4. If we play with a selfless spirit, we can win.
5. If we play in the moment, we can win.[16]

These cultural assumptions and their manifestations would prove crucial during the introduction of the triangle offense.

Implementing the Triangle Offense

The implementation of the triangle offense was stressful for everyone, and it was a year and a half before it was fully in place.[17] During this time, Jackson proved his mettle. He greeted the resistance of Jordan and the uncertainty of the other players with equanimity, convinced that experience would vindicate his strategy.

Not everyone could have done so. Jackson could because of two interlinked skills he had honed over a lifetime: his ability to identify and focus on requirements, and to tolerate diversity tension. The first allowed him to determine what was and wasn't important and to communicate this to his players. The second helped him to stay steadfast by refusing to change course when tension erupted into open conflict.

Focus on Requirements

When responding to a player's behavior, Jackson seemed never to ask, "Do I enjoy this behavior?" Instead, his approach was to remain focused on requirements: "Does this behavior support the sacred journey concept and the Bulls' ability to win?" In managing Rodman, for example, he affirmed the player's ability to deliver double-digit rebounds, remained publicly noncommittal about his extracurricular activities, and discouraged behaviors that got him ejected from the game at the expense of his teammates.[18]

Tolerance of Diversity Tension

Jackson responded similarly to diversity tension between teammates, and between himself and management and players. Those tensions that impaired his ability to meet requirements received careful scrutiny and attention. Those that did not were viewed as less important.

When considering how to deal with those tensions that had to be addressed, Jackson chose his response on the basis of requirements. Implementing the triangle offense was an example. He determined what had to happen and then expected all participants to adjust and adapt to make that happen.

DIVERSITY MANAGEMENT IN ACTION

Phil Jackson handled his basketball team with all the instinctive knowledge of a highly skilled diversity manager. Studying his responses to a few typical diversity situations can be very instructive.

Scenario 1: During the 1992–1993 season, team members appeared to be out of sync with each other. When questioned, captains Cartwright and Jordan told Jackson that some of the players had distanced themselves emotionally from the team.

Response: Jackson encouraged the players to have a Super Bowl party. While the team was together, he talked again of the sacredness of the journey. He reminded players of the internal rewards of such a journey and of the love they had for each other and the game. The players reconnected.[19]

Scenario 2: When Jackson took over as coach, he found a team characterized by a key diversity mixture: one superstar and the "others." This team could not live up to its collective potential.

Response: Jackson's approach was focused on redefining everyone's role. He started by redefining a superstar. It was not, he said, a person who saves the day but rather one who raises the level of everyone's play. He used the structural change required by the triangle offense to place everyone at ground zero as team members. All players had to learn the new system and modify their game. These changes provided a context that had the potential to reunite them as a team.[20]

Scenario 3: Jackson and Horace Grant, who provided much of Chicago's rebounding capability before Rodman, clashed over Grant's unwillingness to play with a tendinitis condition. Grant feared that he might injure himself and compromise his value as a free agent the following year. At first, Jackson responded angrily. He accused Grant of not living up to the team's code of "play hard, play fair, and play now," and told him to stay away until he got his act together. At this point, enormous diversity tension existed between the two.

Response: Jackson dealt with this confrontation by going into a period of self-reflection and discussion with his wife. He concluded that he needed to show Grant the same selflessness and compassion that he expected from him on the court. This perspective allowed him to repair the relationship.[21]

Scenario 4: In games with Detroit, diversity tension and competitiveness often generated anger that distracted the Bulls from their game plan.

Response: Jackson encouraged a nonbelligerent form of competition that called simultaneously for bravery and gentleness. He introduced the Lakota ideal of teamwork and the Taoist principle of rendering an opponent powerless by yielding to his force. He also urged the Bulls not to see every confrontation as a personal test of manhood. Instead, they were to play through confrontational moments.[22]

Scenario 5: In 1995 Jackson brought Dennis Rodman to the team. Rodman, an undeniably talented player, came with considerable potential for disruptive behavior—not a virtue in a team setting, especially one founded on selflessness.

Response: Jackson's approach to Rodman shows a great deal about responding effectively to differences. Clearly Rodman brought to the Bulls a number of differences. Some were directly related to his basketball competencies and were greatly valued. Others were accepted and respected even though they did not explicitly or implicitly contribute anything of value to his basketball game.

The Bulls said, in essence, that they did not wish to change Rodman but simply to access his basketball talent. The diversity and differences Rodman brought were not always of value to the team. Sometimes they simply had to be worked through to get at his talent. This is the essence of what is meant by accepting diversity.

LESSONS TO BE LEARNED

The experience of Phil Jackson and the Chicago Bulls offers some lessons in addressing diversity successfully:

◀ *Clarity is important.* Jackson was clear and specific about his vision of the sacred journey and about the requirements for achieving this vision.

◀ *Shared meanings and purpose are important.* Jackson's concept of the sacred journey offered his players these meanings and purpose, encouraging them to put individual differences in perspective. Those differences were not ignored, but they were considered along with and in the context of similarities.

◀ *Respect, trust, and empathy—the ability to see the other person's perspective—are more important than the kind of chumminess that is often associated with interpersonal harmony.* It is not clear that individual Bulls players liked each other or achieved perfect harmony. It is clear that they respected and trusted each other and were committed to working together on the court.

◀ *Differences must be approached in context.* Jackson neither offered a broad endorsement of nor celebrated differences. He accepted their reality, then responded according to the impact they had on the Bulls. Those that supported achievement of the vision were valued and embraced. Those with no impact on this achievement were conditionally accepted. Those that interfered with achieving the vision were rejected—and were grounds for exclusion from the team.

◄ *Focusing on the moment makes it easier to address diversity effectively.* Clarity about requirements is essential to diversity management. To the extent that people focus on the past or distant future rather than the present, they are likely to be unclear about requirements.

◄ *Individual contributors, not just managers, must be effective in addressing diversity.* The Bulls' success with diversity and its tensions can be attributed to the players as well as to Jackson. Intrateam squabbles appear to have been kept at a minimum, on-court cooperation at a maximum.

◄ *Diversity of all kinds is challenging.* Some have seen Michael Jordan as the epitome of all-around excellence and Dennis Rodman as the prototype of the troublesome player who does not fit in. These observers would predict that Rodman would have presented the greatest diversity challenge. Yet the Bulls' "Jordan problem" experience demonstrates that even "good" diversity is a challenge.

As "head giraffe" of the Chicago Bulls team, Jackson proved to be a master at diversity management. He led his team of powerful and different players to six NBA championships in eight years.

Clearly, some of his success resulted from his respect for and ability to connect with his players. Equally important, however, was his ability to create an organizational environment that empowered each of the players to reach their maximum potential and to do so in pursuit of team as well as personal objectives. Jackson saw parallels between the warrior's journey and life in the NBA.

An additional contribution to Jackson's successful diversity management was his bias toward action learning: analysis, reflection, experimentation, learning. and subsequent action. Addressing diversity is a fluid process. One must be "in the moment." A perception that seemed valid at one time may need to be reassessed. An approach that works in one situation may not work in the next. Flexibility is key. To manage diversity effectively is to remain open to learning and to act on what has been learned.

NOTES

1. Phil Jackson and Hugh Delehanty, *Sacred Hoops: Spiritual Lessons of a Hardwood Warrior* (New York: Hyperion, 1995), p. 4.

2. Ibid., p. 172.

3. Ibid., p. 4.

4. Ibid., p. 89.

5. Ibid., p. 108.

6. Ibid., p. 109.

7. Ibid., p. 112.

8. Ibid., p. 26.

9. Ibid., p. 115.

10. Ibid., p. 4.

11. Bernie Linicicomo, "Disaster Will from This Desperate Move," *Chicago Tribune*, Oct. 3, 1995.

12. Jackson and Delehanty, *Sacred Hoops*, p. 211.

13. Terry Armour, "Bulls Warm Up to 'Worm' Roll Dice, Obtain Rodman for Perdue," *Chicago Tribune*, Oct. 3, 1995.

14. Terry Armour and Sam Smith, "Rodman Likely to Meet With New Teammates," *Chicago Tribune*, Oct. 3, 1995.

15. Jackson and Delehanty, *Sacred Hoops*, pp. 3–7.

16. Ibid.

17. Ibid., p. 102.

18. Sam Smith, "Rodman Situation Is in Good Hands With Jackson," *Chicago Tribune*, Oct. 4, 1996.

19. Ibid., pp. 161–162.

20. Ibid., pp. 84–92.

21. Ibid., pp. 155–156.

22. Ibid., p. 136.

The Making of a Diversity Manager: Bill Smith

4

The story that follows is about a real company and a real person. The names of both have been changed, but not the events. The man we call Bill Smith told his story at a recent gathering of his organization's key managers.

Recently Smith's company has been moving forward in a serious, sustained, multifaceted, and multiyear strategic diversity management process. As the CEO of a subsidiary within the corporation, he must provide leadership for this process in his unit. He believes that his earlier experiences with "diversity" and also his evolution as a "diversity manager" helped prepare him for this task

Bill Smith's Story

While a relatively young man, I worked twice in Plant 6, one of several plants that produced farm machinery products. I served as manufacturing superintendent in 1977 and 1978, left and served in the corporate office, then returned as plant manager in 1980. Both the plant and my preparation for the responsibilities I assumed there were unique.

The resulting experiences had a significant impact on my beliefs about managing people—those different from and similar to me. These experiences also instilled in me an abiding belief in the value of several managerial principles and practices. As such, they have been important in shaping my career.

Manufacturing Superintendent: The First Challenge

Plant 6 was different from the others in several ways. Each of the other plants was regionally based, non-union, and focused on one product line. In contrast, Plant 6 handled parts for all of the different product lines, including a variety of electronic circuit boards and devices, various switches and senders, and tachometers. All required different graphics and dials, and a variety of configurations based on highly variable optional contents. The plant probably had more original equipment parts numbers than all the other plants combined. Frequent model changes and floor space turnovers were typical, as were many new parts numbers, designs, and technologies.

The plant differed in two other ways as well. It was located in a highly unionized area, and was itself a union plant with a complex history of union-management relationships. It was also the lowest-performing plant in the multiplant complex.

My difference was in my background. I had begun my career as an industrial engineer and supervisor, working on cost-reduction programs. I then spent two years as general supervisor of a data processing operation. The two years before going to the plant, I served as a general supervisor of methods engineering, where I focused on assembly line design. What I had not done before arriving at Plant 6 as the manufacturing superintendent was to spend a lot of time in the plants.

The model and parts changes facing the plant in 1977 were even more dramatic than usual. All 1978 farm equipment design, like that of automobiles, was changed in response to the oil shocks of the mid-1970s. The situation was particularly bad in one of our product lines: the flexible cables that connected the instrument cluster to the transmission to get the speed input. The new flex shaft required that we produce an 84-inch cable. This created a major problem. We had an automatic machine that allowed us to convert from one part number to another in about two minutes by changing the cut-off lengths of the machine. But 81-inch cables were the longest it could produce.

The new flex shaft also increased the amount of cable we needed every day. To make matters worse, production engineering had not developed a model change plan for Plant 6 because the flexible cables were low-profit items, and there wasn't much money to spend.

Before I arrived at the plant, I was told that we could build several thousand of these devices at a plant in the southern region. By the time I had been there a month, I knew it couldn't be done. We had to find a way to build them ourselves.

The Management Team

The key players in the efforts to turn this situation around were a management team of seven general supervisors and a production engineer who had been assigned to us.

The production engineer was a white man, as were five of the general supervisors. The production engineer and one of the general supervisors were older and very experienced. The second general supervisor was a young man with a military background who looked as crisp and energetic at the end of a stressful twelve-hour day as he did when he came in.

The third general supervisor was a young manufacturing manager who had been transferred to Plant 6 to help ``fix'' the traditionally inefficient electronics area after proving himself in other plants. This man had, in fact, been so successful as a manufacturing and general supervisor that I'm sure he felt he should have had my job.

The fourth had been sent to Plant 6 after an unsuccessful attempt to gain cross-functional experience at another plant. He had been reassigned to the third-shift operations in Plant 6 as, I suppose, some form of remedial education.

The fifth general supervisor (and sixth team member) was Bob, who had been a general foreman at the northwest region plant, the most geographically remote and least conforming of all the manufacturing plants. Its supervisors marched to their own drums. The plant was known as a successful plant but one whose managers walked on the edge.

Bob was known as a redneck, a cowboy, and a rogue, and a nonteam player as well. He also had what was, to my ears, a strange speech pattern. He had no formal education, no engineering degrees. But he did have a lot of talent. He had been assigned to the plant as a tool engineer to help ''fix'' the disaster in flex shafts. He was there because the lack of preparation for the flex shaft model change had left the head of Production Engineering and my boss's boss too angry to talk directly with each other.

The sixth general supervisor was Pat, a young white woman with a degree in social work. Pat, who had recently been assigned to Plant 6 as general supervisor for Production Control, had some—but not much—experience in production control in the main office.

The seventh general supervisor and eighth team member was Jack, a second-shift general foreman, a forty-something black man with a penchant for extremely fancy three-piece suits and lots of gold jewelry. He had, early in his career, been a union committee man while working for an automobile manufacturing firm. At the time I met him, he was best friends with the shop committee chairman of a 12,000-member local at this firm. He had quite a reputation at the plant.

I felt comfortable with the first four team members and only marginally concerned about the fifth. But the last three left me skeptical. I was particularly concerned about Pat. I didn't say anything. But as I looked around at all the things that were going wrong, I thought, *Why do I have to have the handicap of working with a woman who is a social worker?*

I not only lacked confidence in several members of my crew. I had some doubts about myself. I didn't have an excess amount of management self-confidence, and I was experiencing the personal anxiety and bellyaches a person struggles with each time he gets a new problem.

I knew I was a rookie—a very inexperienced manufacturing person who had been given a responsible job in a very difficult plant. Why, I didn't know. But I assumed it was an experiment. People wanted to know what I would do with all of that.

I also knew that my new crew shared my misgivings. Most of the crew were career manufacturing people, and I correctly assumed they didn't respect me because of my background. I knew that I must manage these people effectively or they would quickly become cynical. I was very self-conscious and a little intimidated about earning their respect.

What kept me going was that I knew I had a job to do. I also knew I had earned a reputation as a problem solver in the data processing department, where I had been a supervisor.

Crew Members in Action

Bob

Bob amply fulfilled my expectations during his first few weeks on the job. Apparently he became frustrated when he couldn't get a desk moved from one area to another using the proper set of rules. He solved his problem by having tradesmen work out of their assigned lines of demarcation to move the desk for him. In the process, he managed to upset the entire skilled trades and engineering organization structure in the main office complex.

What he did sounds trivial now. But this was Michigan, where they had sit-down strikes and machine guns in the 1930s. Even today there are people who remember the abusiveness of management in those early days.

These memories carried consequences. Twenty years ago, union relations in the area were so structured that Bob's actions created a major crisis—as several skilled trades union committee men and my boss and other key executives called to let me know. *So this is what it's going to be like to supervise Bob*, I thought.

I had mixed emotions. On the one hand, I thought, *Man, why did we have to face this so soon?* On the other hand, I admired Bob for serving notice that he was going to get his job done. When the bureaucracy didn't respond, he found a way. On the outside, I said, "Oh dear, this shouldn't have happened." But privately Bob and I had a chuckle. I told him, "Do the best you can not to poke them in the eye."

Once on the job, Bob diligently went to work. It was clear that he understood mechanical devices and floor traditions. He also knew how to work with tradesmen and tool rooms to get things done. He focused first on our inability to produce enough footage of flexible cable per day in our wire winding operation.

Soon he and a young supervisor improved the output in that area greatly.

In the meantime, the crisis in flexible cable assemblies was growing. Things were so bad that we met daily with the general manager and his entire staff. I stood on one side of the view charts while the production control superintendent stood on the other. Together we talked through each day's shipments and promises, and explored plans for avoiding or solving major problems. But no matter what we did, we couldn't get past the inability of the automatic machines to run 84-inch shafts.

The meetings and extreme frustration had been going on for about a month when Bob and the local tool room general supervisor came into my office. They had, they said, a method that would allow us to convert the automatic machines to run 84-inch flexible shafts. "I know that," I said. "The problem is we don't have the six months the engineering department and tool room managers say it will take to do it." The two men stood there and just smiled.

"How long would you need?" I asked.

"One night," they said.

"Do you have any detailed plans, any sketches—anything—that would give people confidence that this plan would work?" I asked.

"All the plans are in my head," Bob replied.

I spent some time learning what I could about the proposal and several hours trying to decide what to do.

Then, during an even grimmer-than-usual afternoon meeting, management pressed us again about what we were going to do. I looked at the general manager and said, "Bob and Bruce say they can convert the automatic machines to run 84-inch flex shafts." The engineering and tool room leaders answered, with some exasperation, "We know that. But it would take lots of money and six months to do it."

I played my trump card: "Bob and Bruce think they can do it in one night."

The room erupted into a combination of laughter and shouting at the ridiculousness of my proposal. I just let the steam blow off and looked across at the general manager. "Well," I said, "we're losing with the strategy we're using now. So what do you say?"

He thought a moment, then looked out at the rest of the group, and said, "Do it."

We all stayed late that night. In my entire career, I have never seen so many skilled tradesmen work so hard on one project. They were literally climbing all around and over that machine from all directions, all working to Bob's plans in his head.

I left to get some sleep. I came back the next morning about an hour before the works manager was due to come see how things were going.

With some trepidation, I asked Bob, "How do things look?"

"Well, we had one problem." *I knew it,* I thought. But then he replied, "A conduit that we thought was just a structural support needed to be cut. When we cut it with the torch, we found that it was full of wires. We also had to do a major rewiring of the machine last night. But we think we're close to having it work."

I know it sounds melodramatic. But just as our works manager walked down the long aisle to the machine and rounded the corner, the machine started to produce its first part.

Bob's butchered job of reconfiguring that machine not only worked the first day, as he had promised. It continued to run and make 84-inch flex shafts during all the critical periods of the start-up and throughout the rest of the model year.

Pat

Pat turned out to be one of the most professional, matter-of-fact people I ever worked with. Her demeanor was neutral but determined and tenacious. In those days, general supervisors were typically crude, table-pounding men. Pat wasn't aggressive. She attacked issues, not people. Her hard work, tenacity, and determination eventually won everyone's respect.

Pat also taught me a lesson I've used repeatedly throughout my career. She had two responsibilities: to get a huge number of purchased materials to us at the time needed and to see that we shipped products to our warehouses on schedule.

One day we were working on a particularly difficult problem—one that involved technical, supply, and execution issues—

just about every kind of problem we could have. I, being an engineer, had looked at the situation time and again to see if we had done everything we could logically do. I was convinced that we had. Yet we were about to fail. Because I thought nothing else could be done, I was resigned to this failure.

As we reviewed the problem, several general supervisors gave extremely logical reasons why they couldn't meet production deadlines, as Pat had requested. I, to my later chagrin, agreed with them. After hearing all that, Pat calmly looked me in the eye and said, "Well, Bill, that's just not good enough."

I didn't know what to say. She was right, of course. The customer had to be served, and we had to find a way. Faced with Pat's unyielding stance, we reexamined our plans and found a way to keep the necessary supply of parts flowing.

Many times since that experience with Pat, people have given me perfectly logical reasons why failure was imminent. At some point, I have simply looked them in the eye and said, "That's just not good enough. Find a way."

Jack

Jack had an air that let you know you didn't want to cross him. Yet for all of his macho characteristics, he was an amazingly warm and charismatic man—the kind of person you want to be your friend.

I never said anything to Jack about his dress, although it made me queasy in the beginning. Eventually it didn't matter. The suits and jewelry were part of what made his character whole. He wouldn't have been Jack if he had been bland.

Besides, behind the flashy exterior, Jack was an extremely solid manager. He trained his staff in the basics of the business and taught them how to get the job done. He followed through with the plans made on the first shift and was a key contributor. He also had an enormous amount of plant savvy and people skills.

These characteristics served him well in an incident that I particularly remember. I was concerned about a young black male supervisor on the third shift. He seemed like a really good man, but his performance was significantly worse than those of supervisors of the other shifts. After trying everything I knew to do, I finally went to Jack and asked if he would be willing to help the young man even though he was not his responsibility.

Within a few weeks, the supervisor had made a miraculous turnaround. His efficiency equaled or exceeded those of the other shifts.

Curious, I asked Jack how he did it: "Did you work with this fellow? He's doing so much better, and I was just curious as to what had happened."

Jack said he had talked with the young man, and the problem had turned out to be simple. Three set-up men had been intimidating him, telling him to do things their way or they would find him outside of work and do him physical harm.

Amazed that this was happening in the plant, I asked, "What did you do?"

"I just found the three men on the way out of work. I told them I had heard rumors that they were intimidating one of our supervisors and that I was going to assume that the rumors were true. I said, 'If anything happens to this supervisor outside of work, I will assume that you three men have done it, and I will have that handled outside of work as well.' "

I think it was Jack's description of how he planned to handle it that convinced the men to back off.

As I got to know Jack better, I tried to talk him into taking assignments on the first shift. I told him it would lead to promotions. But he wasn't interested. He liked what he did, and he knew how to do it. He was truly a contented individual. I came to consider him a great friend.

Plant Manager: The Next Challenge

My experience as plant manager of Plant 6 was as key in shaping my basic management philosophy as my experience as manufacturing superintendent had been in teaching me about people.

It began as inauspiciously as my experience as manufacturing superintendent. My return came the year after a series of miscalculations.

Things were in bad shape. Neither the plant nor the employees had recovered from a difficult year.

My new boss began by telling me I wasn't his first choice for the job. He then put me out into the plant for a week. There I saw firsthand the disorganization, inefficiency, and very low morale. I also saw excessive absenteeism and tardiness, poor work methods, and people reading on the job—in short, an inefficient plant and a disheartened workforce.

At the end of the week, my boss called me: "If you don't turn things around, they're going to close the plant and spread the work among regions that have excess capacity. What's your plan?"

This was a time when managers were preoccupied with job enrichment, becoming the total manager, and heeding the most recent wisdom of the business gurus. But I was uncomfortable with that. "I want to restore discipline," I said. "We need to work on the basics: We'll focus first on housekeeping—assigning a place for everything in the factory to create a safe environment and an element of discipline. We'll focus next on scrap and reject control, absenteeism, efficiency, and not reading on the job. That's all we're going to talk about."

"That's a good place to start," he said, and left me alone.

The rules that followed did not win me friends. The announcement that people couldn't have reading material in the workplace while the line was running was particularly unpopular. Within a week, the union head was in my office telling me I was the worst manager ever. "The rule will hurt morale," he warned. I agreed that it probably would in the short term. But I assured him morale would improve as we worked better and achieved success.

He left, and we worked on the program. I'm not so naive as to think we eradicated reading on all of the shifts. But we achieved a big reduction. It wasn't too big an issue. But it was a point of discipline.

Achieving Success

The team we assembled at Plant 6 was widely viewed as having improved the plant. We got particular credit for our budget performance. It began when I naively made a very optimistic fore-cast about our ability to run efficiently and control expenses for the remainder of the model year. When my boss challenged me, I was too proud to admit I had made a mistake.

When I explained my problem to the general supervisors, they said, "Talk them into getting all of the plant supervisors gold Cross pens and pencils, and we will make the targets." They did, and we celebrated by having a personalized logo designed for our gold Cross pens and pencils and giving them to all fifty members of our team.

What Made It Work?

In reviewing my experiences at Plant 6, I've identified several factors and management principles that helped me to make things work.

The first may be a personal background that equipped me to deal with differences. I grew up in a solidly lower-middle-class family in a small town in central Pennsylvania where all the prejudices held sway. I was an honor student, which could have led to insulation—and isolation. But I played sports, and this was the great equalizer. I was an honor student who enjoyed the social activities of people who bordered on juvenile delinquency. I had black and white friends. My friends were as diverse economically as they were in other arenas.

One thing that made this possible was that my father never showed any prejudice against anybody. He simply did not judge people. I worked for him for several years before graduating from college.

I didn't realize it at the time, but I was developing an appreciation for and acceptance of diversity. Have I had my share of prejudices and biases over the years? Clearly. But I've been re-strained from acting on these biases by my earlier experiences.

Another factor that I believe helped was my ability to estab-lish a work relationship with this talented team that was simultane-ously friendly and participative, and authoritarian. This sounds like a contradiction, but it wasn't. My stance depended on the situa-tion. Sometimes I joined the team and took equal responsibility for trying to find a solution. At other times, I stepped back and evaluated the results. I had to learn case by case which situation called for which response.

This was true of my interactions with individuals as well. At times I was comfortable being a friend and sharing a joke or having a private conversation. At other times, I had to decide on the amount of a raise or the content of an evaluation. Other situations called for a one-minute reprimand—and a reaffirmation of the person's value as soon as this made sense. My goal wasn't to be consistent in every situation. It was to establish a *pattern* that was consistent. Over the years, this interpersonal style has seemed to serve me well.

My decision to focus on the basics also contributed to our success. This belief has been reconfirmed time and again. If you have a problem that's very basic at its root, you just kid yourself by working on tangential problems and making yourself happy because you're active.

Lessons Learned

I have always been a habitual first-impression former. When faced with a situation or individual, I cannot help jumping to a conclusion about evaluating the situation or person. What I have learned is that some of my most important life lessons and accomplishments have come from having first impressions be wrong.

I still form first impressions, but I'm much more careful about acting on them. If I do act quickly, I keep my antennas up for new data. My first impression of Bob was partially right, partially wrong. My first impression of Pat was wrong, as it was of Jack. My first impressions of a lot of people have been wrong. A boss of mine whom I greatly respect once told me, "You don't ever know people. They reveal themselves over a period of time."

I've also learned that I must trust others. It's one of those things I've grown into as I have gotten through crises of bigger and bigger proportions by counting on others.

Finally, I learned to value the consistency that follows from staying focused on the requirements of the situation. The higher the level of the leader, the greater the consequences of wasted motions. You can't jerk the organization around with a new program every year, a new idea every day. An organization gets a certain momentum. You must get it going in the right direction and have the patience to see it through.

Lessons Carried Forward

My work in recent years has given me ample opportunity to use the lessons I learned at Plant 6. It has created new challenges and taught me new lessons as well.

A few years ago, I moved to an industry that is about two decades behind the rest of the country in diversity awareness. The organization I went to had some diversity awareness with respect to minorities but practically none with respect to women.

One important barrier was a strong shared belief that a woman could not be a service engineer, that being a demanding, lonely, and sometimes dangerous job. Yet experience in this job is traditionally essential to career advancement. The result was that although salaried women were represented in level 8, the highest classified level, they were not represented in the unclassified or higher levels.

During my first year, I had enough other problems to prevent me from focusing on that issue. Then I attended a meeting where we reviewed the results of some catalyst studies and were asked to reflect on the results and make recommendations. I was intrigued but felt I lacked sufficient information, so I set out to get some.

In early 1997, I called a meeting of a diagonal slice of women in our U.S. and Canadian plant sites. Out of those meetings came two significant things.

I was touting the benefits of the human resources management committee to a collection of eighth-level and substaff department heads whose purpose was to make decisions that affected workers at lower organizational levels. A woman stood up and asked, "How many women are on that committee?" I had to admit I didn't know. A participant who did know spoke up. "There aren't any," she said. Within a month, we appointed a proportionate number of women to that committee. So that was the first thing.

We also decided that a women's organization was the best

forum for making progress on issues of unique interest to women. We had such an organization in Canada but nothing like that in the United States.

A core group of fifteen to twenty U.S. women began meeting to select their leadership, agenda, and proposed budget in preparation for forming an organization. They held their first total membership meeting several months ago. The women did the work: the organizing, the surveys, and everything else. I've met with the group several times.

It hasn't always been easy to work with the women's groups or to accept the decisions that came out of their work. In Canada, for example, we decided to eliminate core hours from our flex rules and allow for the banking of hours. I'll give it a try, but I don't think it's right. It's important to be flexible, but flexibility must take place within the context of what's good for the business.

I told the group, "We all have one thing in common. None of us will have a job if we don't compete. I'm not working with you because I'm a social activist. I've become convinced that job parity and attention to women's issues are essential if we are to remain competitive."

I always let them know I'm in this because there's a business interest. It helps them to understand that I'm going to be consistent in making judgments about what's best for the business. Sometimes what benefits the business benefits them as well. Sometimes what benefits the business takes some sacrifice on their part.

Staying In Touch With Principles and People

As anyone's position in the organization rises, it's harder to keep from getting isolated. Yet it's essential not to do so. Working with the women's groups is one way I stay in touch with the management principles that inform my career and the people in the organization.

Another way that I do this is to meet every month with a diagonal slice of union and salaried employees in both of our plant locations. Facing these people monthly causes me to evaluate my positions and consistency on an ongoing basis.

This kind of ongoing evaluation and consistency are, I believe, the key to the effective leadership of a dynamic and diverse workforce.

SMITH AS EFFECTIVE DIVERSITY RESPONDENT

Bill Smith's ability to turn around a declining plant under difficult conditions was, in large part, due to four personal characteristics:

1. His focus on meeting requirements
2. His willingness to put aside initial misgivings and to work with whomever was available
3. His ability to observe himself and his responses to situations and people
4. His ability to learn from experiences and other people

Clearly Smith didn't go looking for diversity. He, like the vast majority of managers, bumped into it on the way to doing his job. Equally clearly, he didn't think in terms of "diversity mixtures." He didn't know the term existed. Yet he intuitively responded to these mixtures in ways that allowed him to meet requirements—and to learn about himself and others in the process.

To work together successfully, Smith and his direct reports first had to address the diversity mixture that created internal tension: the difference between the attributes of the direct reports or manager they would have liked to have and the one(s) they had been given.

Smith was a technically educated, conservative white male who relied on logic to solve problems. He would have preferred subordinates who were like himself. His direct reports included people who had little education but much experience, relied on intuition to solve problems, and were demographically different in race, gender, and social class.

Smith's direct reports would have preferred a highly experienced manufacturing manager. They were given an inexperienced and, from their perspective, poorly prepared one.

What allowed them to work together productively? Most

important, perhaps, was their shared understanding that they had no choice. If they didn't succeed in turning the plant around, it would close.

Also important was Smith's ability to see himself as part of a manager-subordinate diversity mix. He identified differences and similarities in education, credentials, problem-solving approaches, race, gender, social class, and age both among his subordinates and among these subordinates and himself. He appears to have understood that he was as "different" or "idiosyncratic" as they were.

Smith's intuitive understanding of diversity management and diversity mixtures allowed him to provide adequate leadership in shaping up the plant while leaving himself open to learning and using the ideas and solutions of his subordinates. He interacted with both direct reports and others with a diversity mix of roles that included friend, judge, disciplinarian, dispenser of rewards, supplicant, decision maker, and participatory colleague. In each instance, his choice of role was meant to help achieve the business requirement.

Smith was as unfamiliar with the term *mutual adaptation* as with the idea of diversity management. "I felt I had a job to do," he says, describing the motivation for his behaviors. Yet in focusing on identifying and addressing business requirements, assuming an appropriate mixture of managerial roles, and building on the strengths of a diverse group of people, he exemplified the use of this action option. He was, in this respect, a man ahead of his time.

🦒 5 🦒
Diversity Effectiveness: The Challenges for Head Giraffes

Head giraffes, as leaders of their organizations, have responsibilities that elephants and other giraffes do not. Many of these responsibilities have an effect, sometimes direct and sometimes indirect, on the quality of diversity management in the company. The decisions that head giraffes make on a daily basis filter into the organization's culture and to a large degree determine whether diversity management can take hold.

Phil Jackson and Bill Smith are highly effective diversity managers. On the surface it can look as if they are highly intuitive in the way they go about it.

Yet this is not so. It is true that a significant part of their diversity effectiveness flows from their personal sense of the importance of empowerment and respect. Yet to this they add a focus on requirements and an ability to create an organizational culture that both allows all organizational participants to meet requirements and encourages them to want to do so.

Their experiences are unique and at the same time universal. The lessons embodied in them can provide a diversity effectiveness map for all head giraffes.

BIG-PICTURE CONCERNS

The task of detailing the big picture falls uniquely to head giraffes. The big picture they paint provides context for all organizational activities. The clearer the picture is, the more on target decisions can be in the service of the organization's objectives. The more compelling the picture is, the more likely that a diverse workforce will pull together to achieve these objectives.

To create this picture and ensure that it continues to evolve as circumstances require, head giraffes must regularly consider these questions:

- How is the corporation's environment changing?
- What should be the company's mission, vision, strategy, and culture?
- How should power be distributed among organizational participants?
- How shall we ensure that our diverse workforce functions effectively to achieve organizational objectives?
- How shall we satisfy the requirements of stakeholders, as a means of maintaining organizational viability?

Phil Jackson demonstrates how head giraffes can do this. His clarity about the environment, the organization's mission, and himself has been critical to his ability to field a championship team by providing a framework within which to make decisions and take action.

The Organization's Environment

One useful way to come to grips with an increasingly complex external environment is to compare the current environment to that of the past and to the one that is likely to exist in the future. A head giraffe's failure to recognize how the environment has evolved and is likely to evolve can mean failure for the company.

The managerial task here is threefold:

1. To understand how the environment is changing
2. To seek to understand and communicate the significance of these changes
3. To use this information when making decisions regarding the organization

Bill Smith had no difficulty understanding his environment. It was one of crisis that threatened his organization and, if he failed to perform, his personal viability as well. This clarity helped him to focus on requirements and be receptive to nontraditional workers and approaches.

Mission, Vision, Strategy, and Culture

The mission is the organization's fundamental purpose. Its mission statement answers the questions: "Why are we here?" "What are we endeavoring to do?" Articulating this mission is a task for the head giraffe.

Head giraffes must consciously ensure that their organization's mission evolves with its environment by continuously reviewing past, present, and possible future missions in the light of environmental realities. This mission, once identified, must then be communicated and given meaning.

Phil Jackson did a superb job of this. He thought about how to make meaning of basketball and its realities within the context of a bigger picture. Ultimately Jackson developed an understanding of basketball in the context of spirituality. By communicating this understanding to his team, he transformed a mission—to win a championship each season—into a "sacred journey."

Jackson's sacred journey reflects the reality that the more meaning a company's mission has for its participants, the more they can commit. A mission with meaning strengthens the individual-organization bond.

Vision is closely linked to mission. An organization's vision statement specifies what achievement of its mission would look like in action. The key head giraffe's task here is to flesh the vision out and communicate it effectively to rank-and-file members. The more vivid and detailed the vision is, the more likely that organizational participants will understand and commit to it.

The third component of the big picture is strategy. Strategy determines how successful the organization will be relative to its competition. It specifies what will be done to secure competitive advantage in pursuit of mission and vision. Without a clear mission and vision, it is impossible to develop an effective strategy.

The final big-picture component of concern to the head giraffe is the organization's culture. Culture consists of the basic assumptions—prescriptions for success—that drive an organization, and the practices, systems, structures, and other components that flow from them.

Organizations that hope to change direction must be willing to change their basic assumptions as well. The head giraffe must take the lead here. Phil Jackson's experience illustrates how one head giraffe developed and communicated the basic assumptions that constitute the heart of organizational culture.

The difficulty for head giraffes who desire to encourage change is that in established business organizations, corporate culture is so pervasive and taken for granted that it can be hard to identify and even harder to change. However, as external environments become more unpredictable and opportunities greater for companies willing and able to take strategic risks, head giraffes can no longer take the big-picture variables as givens. They too will be expected to change organizational assumptions and environments as needed.

Distribution of Power

Head giraffes must ensure that the distribution of power (ability to influence) exists where it is needed for the success of the organization, now and in the future. This is a head giraffe task.

When Bill Smith assumed his roles, the distribution of power was not appropriate for the success of the organization. Tradition and hierarchical arrangements placed the bulk of power in his hands, yet he knew relatively little about the operations for which he had responsibility. Given the urgency of performance, this allocation was in need of change.

A more appropriate allocation would reflect at a minimum the empowerment of Smith and his direct reports. Neither ideology nor personal preference determined this desired state. It was dictated by the requirements of the moment. Smith modified the power allocation in two ways: He listened to and supported his managers and asked for assistance when he needed it.

Phil Jackson also inherited a major power distribution challenge, one popularly known as the "Jordan problem." Jackson attacked this challenge on two fronts. He redefined what it meant to be a "great" player, and he adopted an offense that required the involvement of all team members.

Both men addressed their problem by empowering others; in neither case did empowerment disenfranchise anyone.

Managers sometimes feel that empowerment will do this. They can be particularly fearful that to empower others is to disempower themselves. This is especially true in circumstances such as Smith's, where managers know less than their subordinates. In such situations, it can seem as if empowering others will lead to a loss of managerial control. Yet Smith's experience suggests otherwise. The more he empowered, the more effective and respected he became as a manager. He gained rather than lost power.

Integrating Diverse Workers

Head giraffes bear the main responsibility for ensuring that the parts function in an integrated fashion around organizational objectives. They must, for example, ensure that employees who are similar and different in many ways can work together. This is key to their efforts. The workforce diversity mixture can contribute enormously in pursuit of organizational objectives. It can also result in chaos.

A key to making this mixture work is to remain clear about the difference between requirements and preferences and acting on this clarity. EDR head giraffes set the stage for assimilation around requirements by being clear about the kind and amount of diversity that can be accepted. At the same time, they anticipate and accept diversity around nonrequirements and are prepared for the tensions this diversity can create.

They understand that surface similarities and differences do not necessarily tell the whole story as well. Bill Smith's first impression of his direct reports gave him cause for concern. Yet as he worked with these people, he discovered that surface differences hid the commonality of solid business judgment and skills. Jackson looked beyond Dennis Rodman's differences to see unique skills that could be used in pursuit of a championship. This allowed him to access Rodman's talent.

Stakeholder Concerns

All organizations are responsible to a mixture of stakeholders—people and entities with a stake in the enterprise's viability. By its very nature, this group is diverse. A unique role of the head giraffe is to provide leadership in managing this diversity mix.

Key components include stockholders, the head giraffe, managers, employees, customers, vendors, and communities. EDR head giraffes seek to understand each component's agenda, needs, and requirements. Their task is to integrate the organization's and stakeholders' needs. To do this, they must ensure that each stakeholder's involvement and commitment are at the levels necessary for attaining the organization's objectives.

Managing this diversity mixture is a critical aspect of the head giraffe's role. The organization does not belong to any one group of stakeholders, and disenchantment on the part of any key stakeholders can have significant consequences. The notion of stakeholders captures the complexity and diversity inherent in the head giraffe's role.

HEAD GIRAFFE AS CHIEF DIVERSITY MANAGER

As the senior executive of the organization, the head giraffe is the chief manager of diversity issues. As the head giraffe gains in diversity effectiveness, the organization as a whole gains, as do all its participants—at least those who are paying attention. Because of this position of leadership, some of the most fundamental issues of diversity rest on the shoulders of the head giraffe.

◀ *How do we create a house that engages both giraffes and elephants?* On their own, giraffes and elephants have tended to cooperate in building houses that work for all only in situations where there is a crisis, a strong overarching mission, or a dominating win-win theme. Building one house for both works best when it is a "mission house" designed specifically to foster achievement of a given mission. Holding that mission firm, and using it to lead, is where the head giraffe comes in. The overriding question becomes, "Will this belief, or practice, or procedure contribute to achieving our mission?"

A true mission house works for giraffes and elephants who are committed to the mission. Giraffes and elephants with other agendas will find this house inhospitable. Those unable to support the mission presumably will leave. Those assessed as being unwilling or unable to support it will be asked to leave.

◀ *Do giraffes really have a place in that house?* Some giraffes treat this issue as a major concern. They see the world as a win-lose proposition. They fear that accommodations that make the house more engaging to elephants will make it less so to giraffes. Organizational leaders, the head giraffes, hold the key here. They know they cannot afford to erect barriers or disenfranchise any group. They must instead empower all who work for them.

In true mission houses, leaders assume that everyone is qualified to contribute. Their task is to foster and access those potential contributions. They operate in the inclusive, not exclusive, mode; the empowerment, not disenfranchisement, mode. Indeed, the objectives in these settings will be to create an environment where all feel empowered and engaged.

◀ *Is it possible for giraffes and elephants to trust each other and their organizations in the midst of pioneering change?* Yes. But it will take considerable effort to establish and maintain this trust. Once again, head giraffes lead the way. They need to establish a climate of learning, where it is acceptable for people to acknowledge that they don't have all the answers with respect to diversity management. Even the head giraffes themselves need to admit this. In some organizations, head giraffes act as if it would be grossly inappropriate to admit a need to learn. They attempt to bluff and muddle through instead. But the more they do, the more disillusioned the employees become.

◀ *Just how far do we need to go to accommodate elephants?* As far as is necessary to achieve the company's mission, keeping always in mind the notion of true requirements. Head giraffes have a bit of an edge here, for they can be expected to see the business motive for diversity immediately. This allows them to put differences in context.

Context is everything. To solidify this idea, consider two anecdotes.

The head of a department looked up from his desk one day and saw a male employee wearing a ponytail walk by. His gut reaction was, "No way." He stood up and headed for his door to tell the man the ponytail had to go. Just at that moment, the department head's boss happened by. He pointed to the pony-tailed man and commented, "That fellow does a great job. I didn't realize he was in your section. We need to make sure we keep him." This executive came face-to-face with the differences between personal preferences and job requirements. The employee more than met requirements; he was doing an excellent job.

The second incident involved a company's CEO and his direct reports, who had a strategic planning session. At the end of the session, the CEO offered some closing comments. Here's what he said:

"I've been sitting here thinking about requirements. The world is changing, our industry is changing, our company is changing, and I'm not certain we know what our requirements are. For example, we have this requirement that if you are going to be in senior management, you must have a wife, and she must fit a certain profile. Is that a requirement? I'm not sure. We also have this requirement that says if you want to be selected for senior management, you have to be known by senior management—not just in the context of work, but also in the context of golf. But now I'm thinking, what about our young people who don't play golf and, furthermore, don't care to learn?"

At this point one of the participants interjected, "That's their tough luck!"

"No," the CEO said firmly. "That's *our* tough luck! It means we can't access talent, even proven talent, just because it will not get on the golf course."

◀ *How do we counter giraffe backlash?* Three things can counter giraffe backlash: leadership from the top, communication of the business case, and continuing dialogue. All originate with the head giraffe.

Head giraffes must demonstrate expertise and commitment. Giraffes who believe their leaders lack these characteristics will resist the diversity management effort. They will see it at best as a waste of their time and at worst as a detriment to their welfare. Leaders who communicate the business case for diversity management help to dispel skepticism that this is the "program of the month" or only a minor concern. They also help giraffes, especially stakeholders, to see the benefits of diversity management for themselves. The business case counters the belief that diversify is a moral or social issue for the exclusive benefit of elephants.

Adopting a definition of diversity that includes everyone as part of the mix is helpful as well. If giraffes are part of, as opposed to outside of, the diversity mix, that which promotes diversity works to their good.

Encouraging giraffes to use the diversity concepts to address less emotion-laden mixtures can help prevent backlash too. It is easier to learn and apply the concepts where emotional engagement and intensity are missing. Giraffes can apply the insights gained from these experiences to their "passion" mixtures.

Dialogue among giraffes and elephants can also reduce backlash. The process is to explore similarities as well as differences and their resulting tensions. The purpose is to find a basis for working together to achieve shared objectives.

Head giraffes can help by creating structured settings for candid exchanges or pleas for dialogue. The speaker says, in effect, "Look, we need to talk. I feel victimized and disenfranchised." Useful conversation can follow.

How can we be sure dialogue is truly effective? Dialogue is conversation with a purpose. It is in service of a mission. If it is to be effective, participants must possess a clear and vivid grasp of this mission. The operating question becomes, "Given our mission and our similarities, differences, and related tensions, how and where can we collaborate?"

Identifying the requirements associated with the mission is

essential too, for these requirements form the basis for collaboration. Without clear-cut requirements, dialogue can center around traditions, personal preferences, and conveniences.

Sophistication about differences is critical to the dialogue process too. Diversity-savvy participants identify which differences are potentially of great value, conditionally acceptable, and unconditionally not acceptable. They make these distinctions on the basis of how the differences will affect mission and requirements.

To do so, they must be willing to accept differences with which they disagree or about which they have negative feelings. They must, in effect, be willing to work together in the midst of significant diversity tension.

Finally, a learning mind-set can facilitate dialogue by helping to remind participants that exploration is an important part of the process. Participants without this learning mode will attempt to convert, convince, or prevail, not to explore and evaluate ideas that differ from their own. Their personal agendas will take precedence over those of the collective entity.

All of these realities—mission, real requirements, acceptance of differences and tensions—show themselves in the day-to-day interactions of all the giraffes and elephants in the organization. But they begin with the leadership and diversity skills of the head giraffe. Diversity effectiveness starts at the top.

A MODEL FOR DIVERSITY MATURITY

We expect the leaders of our organizations to lead: to define the company's mission and vision, articulate it with passion to inspire everyone else, create strategies to enact the vision in the marketplace, and shape the underlying climate within which all these elements come together as people go about the day-to-day doing of their job.

In fulfilling these aspects of their responsibilities, leaders are attending to some of the critical aspects of what we have defined as diversity effectiveness. Internalizing the mission, paying attention to the business motive, and focusing on requirements are integral concerns for the leaders. Leaders also, by their nature, tend to be people who have thought carefully about their own goals and desires, and shaped a personal mission for achieving them.

Thus, where head giraffes are concerned, it's reasonable to take as a given that they know well these aspects of diversity effectiveness and put them into play every day, instinctively or systematically and deliberately. True leadership in the arena of diversity comes from their attending to the aspects that are not part of their daily picture, but incorporated through serious reflection. In this regard they are true pioneers of diversity, and by their actions and attitudes they serve all members of the organization as models of diversity effectiveness.

When employees see that the head giraffe takes responsibility for his or her own role in diversity management by clear statements and action; when they watch the head giraffe moving smoothly through complexity without losing control; when they realize that the head giraffe has no difficulty accepting differences where those differences have no impact on business requirements; when they notice that the head giraffe is not debilitated by diversity tension; when they come to understand, by watching the head giraffe in action, the full meaning of diversity—then the head giraffe has fulfilled what may in the long run be a leader's most crucial role: to show others the way.

PART THREE
Elephants in Action

IT would be easy to define elephants as all those who are not white males. But it would also be incorrect. That definition would miss much of the complexity and subtlety that define elephant status.

Elephants are people in other people's houses or in houses that don't work for them. They are outsiders.

The elephant experience is universal. All of us, including white males, function as elephants at certain times and in certain settings.

A remembered "elephant" experience for many of us, for example, is the first holiday we celebrated at our in-laws' house. No matter how kind the people or how determined they were to make us feel comfortable, there were numerous reminders that this was not our house. Open the presents in the evening? Our family always waited until morning. Carve the turkey before it went to the table? Where was their sense of drama? We were uncomfortable. We wanted to please. We couldn't figure out why they didn't do things "right." Yet *we* were the outsider.

At the heart of the elephant experience, even in this minor example, is the felt sense that this is not our house, and we don't know the rules for getting along in it.

The example also makes clear that elephant status is not necessarily determined by ethnicity, race, or gender. Many other factors can trigger the elephant experience. Some of the ones that often show up in organizations include these:

- *Age*. Those who are younger or older than the norm in their company often feel like outsiders. They worry that their productivity will be questioned and their contributions undervalued.
- *Physical ability*. When people who do strenuous physical labor experience declining physical ability as the result of age or injury, they can assume an elephant status. The environment no longer works for them.
- *Physical appearance*, such as extremes of height and weight, or other unusual physical characteristics. Research routinely demonstrates that "tall is better" in many settings. Overweight people are ascribed elephant status in organizations aspiring to achieve a certain look.
- *Education*. Those whose educational attainment differs greatly from their colleagues can feel like outsiders.
- *Work location*. Employees who don't work where the action is can feel that they are in someone else's house. People in the field often report feeling like second-class citizens.
- *Work experience*. When a company with a strong history of promoting from within changes to hiring outside people with experience, these new employees report feeling like outsiders. They often have difficulty in learning their new culture.
- *Acquired status*. Employees who join a parent corporation after their own is acquired often feel they are in someone else's house.
- *Laborer status*. Where employees sense they are in management's house, they seek to form unions to advance the remodeling of the house.
- *Administrative status*. Administrative and clerical staff often feel that they are second-class citizens and have little or no opportunity to become first-class participants.
- *Functional status*. In many organizations, functions and departments have differential status. When one function

or department commands preferential status, those not in this area feel like second-class citizens.

🐘 *Opinions.* People who hold personal views that differ markedly from those of work cohorts can feel like outsiders. Those who believe differently and try to change others can evoke strong reactions.

One other important lesson is obvious from this list: a person's status can shift from issue to issue and from setting to setting. Even in their own work setting, people are almost never exclusively elephants or giraffes. Making assumptions about someone from one setting to the next is as grievous a stereotype as any other kind of prejudice.

6

The Assimilated Elephants: Ray and Carol

Ray's Story

I'm a thirty-five-year-old Mexican American man. I've been with this large family-owned home improvement retail chain for nineteen years. I joined the company in my senior year of high school, worked throughout my college years, and then stayed on after that.

I was a bagger, a checker, and a night stocker before going into the store management training program. After that, I made about fourteen moves in nine years. I became a service director, an assistant store director, and a store director in a very small rural town. Following that, I was a store manager for a small store in Phoenix. I then became a department supervisor, helping to supervise seventeen departments in a 200-square-mile area. My last promotion was to this position. I'm the store director of a large store in Phoenix.

I like my job. It gives me a certain quality of life because I control my own schedule. I work the fifty hours the job requires, but I can basically work them in the five days that I choose.

Growing up, I never dreamed I'd make the home improvement retail business my career. I applied here because my parents said they would continue to give me an allowance if I got a job. I thought I'd outsmart them, so I put in one application. I made sure nobody was watching when I turned it in, and I walked off. My future brother-in-law hired me.

It took me a long time to appreciate store operations. I've always liked numbers, and I really liked working at a desk. But as I got further into my career here and was exposed to the different areas, I couldn't see myself working at a desk anymore. I enjoyed working with people too much.

As I grew, I was given two awards recognizing me as an exemplary employee. After going into management, I received two "excellence in management" awards as well. I was recognized by people not so much because of the things I did but because of the relationships I had.

It is important to me to see employees grow because my success stems from their success. I come from a family that values teaching and education. To my surprise, the work I do here allows me to combine my interests in teaching and helping people with my financial side.

I hadn't expected retail operations to be the way it is. I hadn't known how complex it could be, how much there is to learn, or how interesting I'd find it. I only wish I had realized sooner that this was going to be my calling. I might have moved up faster and been able to help more people.

The Company

This is a family-oriented business, one that is concerned with quality of life and with the individual's growth and well-being. They believe that success starts at home, and it carries over into the business. For example, when my dad got sick about seven years ago, I was living about three hours from where he lived. I asked the company to move me back to the store there, and without hesitation, it did.

It's also an aggressive company, one that changes in order to stay ahead. Management has high standards, and expects to achieve double-digit sales growth that is profitable.

There have been times when the company's family orientation and its aggressiveness have not mixed well. For a time the company forgot its people orientation in pursuit of profits. People began to get the impression that they were seen only as numbers.

Then somebody realized that people had to take the com-

pany where it was going. So they went back to the family environment. People started saying, "This is the company we
remembered, the one we really enjoyed."

I think I can be successful in this organization. For me, success
is being happy in the job I'm doing. It's not so much what position
I hold. I feel successful if I'm able to help a number of people and
watch them grow. I like the dark horse, the Cinderella story where
you give someone an opportunity he or she has never had before. I also want to be successful in the financial operation.

The Ingredients of Success

Understanding of Diversity

Several things have helped me to be successful here. The first
may be my understanding of diversity. To me, diversity is nothing
more than individuality and respect. When my company offered
diversity training, I asked myself, "What's the big deal?" It surprised me that everybody didn't understand it. Maybe the word
diversity hides the meaning. Maybe we should just talk about respect for individuality.

I've seen people in this organization struggle with diversity,
and that irritates me. I think there's a real misunderstanding of
what diversity is. People keep the idea that diversity is about
black or white, male or female. All it is is respect for individuality.

Part of the problem is that we're so caught up in political
correctness. When I grew up, we called each other Mexican or
black or white, and we respected that. I don't understand why
people can't see, "You don't have to like me. Just respect me
for who I am." "You don't have to like how I think. Just respect
me because I think." "You don't have to like what I do. Just respect that I have the ability to do."

I learned about diversity from my earliest days. Both of my
parents were born in the United States, and English is my first language. However, my grandparents were from Mexico. They understood English, but out of respect, we spoke Spanish when we
went to their houses. As a result, we all learned to speak Spanish.

I grew up in a low-income neighborhood. An African American family lived on one side of us, an Anglo American family on

the other. Across the street from us was an Asian American family. We understood that each of us was different. However, we also noticed a lot of similarities. And we learned that you couldn't tell very much about people by how they look on the outside.

Although we came from different cultures, we often thought alike, but just because we thought a lot alike didn't mean we always saw eye to eye. We had to get a grasp of who each individual was. We didn't worry so much about color, race, and gender. There was really a sincere appreciation and respect for each person's individuality. Every person had strengths and gifts, and you could learn from anybody.

When I was five, for example, we had a small cement area to the side of our house that had two basketball hoops. The older kids would call me over when they needed an extra player. I was about four feet tall, and they all looked like six-footers. Still, they appreciated my efforts.

I've carried what I learned in my neighborhood into the workplace. I work in a locality that straddles the line between the city and country. People from both the country and the city work in the store, and I can see the differences. They differ in the terms they use, whether they have long hair or short, whether they have tattoos or not. We have people who have earrings, people who are tall, short, young, old. The morning shift is basically older adults; the afternoon shift is basically high school students. What's neat is when you mix them together during the middle of the day.

Before this store, I worked in several other locations within the area. The customers in one location focused on price. In another location, they focused on quality. In one very diverse and sophisticated location, they focused on everything: price, quality, and service. The management training process gave us experience in high- and low-income areas, in predominantly minority areas and predominantly Anglo American areas. We had to know what people in each area wanted because we had to give them what they wanted, not what we wanted to sell them.

When I look at diversity, I look at what a person brings to the table, whether it's an opportunity or the way he or she thinks and does things. It's just an appreciation for who the person is and his or her uniqueness and ability to do the job. When I look at diverse employees, I look at what they can give to our store.

Comfort With Change

Another thing that has helped me to be successful is my comfort with change. When I was young, change was easy because we were always given the opportunity to make mistakes. There was always support. "Try this thing you've never done before." "Make an attempt, and if it doesn't work, that's okay." My father encouraged me at least to try things so that I could open my eyes to other opportunities. For example, he was a fisherman, and I couldn't see being a fisherman because I didn't believe in taking a life, even if it was a worm. He said, "Give it a try." I never would have tried fishing had I not known it was okay not to like it. I love fishing.

That's part of receiving change. My upbringing taught me that I could make a million mistakes, and I wasn't failing. My parents always said, "If you try and you don't succeed, it's not failing. It's successfully not accomplishing." There was always success in that piece. They allowed my sisters and me to make all the mistakes we needed to as long as we never made the same one twice.

There was a time at work when I had to step out of the box, take the quantum leap. And I thought, "If I order all of this product and I don't sell it, I'm in trouble." But my managers said that wasn't true. They would find a way to help me get rid of the product. So my home training and my work tie in.

Confidence and Ambition

I learned confidence and ambition from my father as well. When he was in the service, he earned a stripe that was given to only one person in the United States that year. He taught us that success isn't about race and ethnicity. It is about how well you present yourself and perform.

The Help of Others

One of the best things that happened to my career occurred just after I had left the rural store and came to Phoenix. The district manager approached me and said, "I've been watching you work, and I'd like to give you an opportunity."

The more I worked for this man, the more I liked him. He put me in the management training program. He gave me my first department and my first store. But what I appreciated most was that he coached and taught and trained. He would say, "Let me show you how it's done; you show me you can do it, and then go out and do it." That's how I learned that this job could be one that could help people in the business and teach them skills they could use in their personal life.

At the time I met this man, I was very immature. But working with him, I began to realize that there is more to life than just making money. It's how to work with people, how to accept who they are, how to become a coach and teacher yourself so that you can help develop people and give them the same type of experience that I have had. He retired two years ago, and it was probably one of the saddest times in my life.

I also worked for other managers who took me under their wing. The managers who cared for me also taught me how to overcome one of my biggest challenges. I was really good at getting along with everybody, but I didn't know the conflict management piece. It was hard for me to give constructive criticism when people weren't doing their job.

I learned that through a supervisory class and individual coaching. My bosses would say, "We're going to deal with this situation, and we want you to sit in on the meeting and watch how we handle it." I'd watch, and they'd take care of it. Then one of my bosses said, "It's your turn. I will be here, and I'll help you if you get stuck." Another boss said, "You're new, and you're going to make a million mistakes. Just don't make the same one twice." That sounded like what I had heard at home.

One reason I appreciated these people so much is that in the past I had worked with people who didn't think my thoughts were important. These people appreciated what I had to say even when I wasn't in a managerial position.

Diversity-Related Tensions

I truly believe that people in our organization are given opportunities based on performance. I've never been given a position that I didn't deserve, and there were times when others got positions that I knew I didn't deserve. I went from being a service manager in 1989 to being a store manager in 1993, so the opportunity was there. I just needed to take that and perform.

Others may not agree. But I see a company that gives the opportunity and a group of employees who have taken it. It seems as if maybe more of the Anglo Americans have taken advantage, but the opportunity is there for everybody. This group of people just chose to take the opportunity to perform.

Not everybody understands that. It's one way I know that people are still confused about diversity. This confusion has created some problems for me. Right before I got my first unit, I had worked on a special project. To do this, I had gone from being a store manager to being a department manager. People who didn't know this thought I had gone from being a department manager to a store manager. If that had been true, I would have skipped some steps.

These people believed, based on their understanding of diversity, that I got the job to help out with the numbers because there weren't enough Mexican American individuals in the store manager position. I know better. The person who tapped me for that position made it very clear that his selection had nothing to do with my being a Mexican American male or with us being friends. It was based on performance. Knowing that made the rumors easier to deal with. But the bad part was that I got a lot of negative comments from other Mexican Americans. They said, "You don't understand. You're being picked because you just happen to be the right guy in the right place." That was really hard to listen to.

Commitment to the Company

Even after I graduated from college, I wasn't sure I wanted to work for this company. While I was in college, I had worked for some people who weren't very good leaders. I had gotten the misperception that that was the way most managers were, and that was a big disappointment.

My contact with a number of caring managers has changed my perceptions and increased my commitment to this organization. I just kept getting one manager after the other who was people-oriented but ran a successful operation, so I knew it could be done.

That was what helped me to decide, "This is the business I want to stay in," because there are people out there who will recognize hard work and effort and appreciate those attributes.

RAY AS EFFECTIVE DIVERSITY RESPONDENT

Ray reports that he has secured a career he enjoys with a company he admires. He is satisfied with his company, work, and career progress. At this time, he is a contented man.

He also notes that he has not always felt the same. And, indeed, his organization has faced lawsuits based on alleged discrimination. The company has responded by working hard to correct the situation and has engaged in vigorous representation and diversity management efforts.

Ray's Diversity Maturity

Ray demonstrates a major strength that bodes well for his ability to become an effective diversity respondent, should he decide to do so: he understands himself and his requirements well. He is aware of how his upbringing has influenced his personality and current requirements and his assimilation decision.

Accepts Responsibility

Ray accepts personal responsibility for getting along with others. But he sees differences as something that shouldn't matter and acts as if they don't. This view could leave individuals who value their demographic and personal differences to experience him as indifferent to their uniqueness. It does prevent him from asking how he might help his organization to address diversity more effectively. At present, he is not aware that he should accept this responsibility.

Demonstrates Conceptual Knowledge

Ray's concept of diversity as respect for individuality can appear at first glance to be "right on." Yet his conversation about diversity suggests that he is loathe to acknowledge differences with which he might disagree. His memories suggest a childhood neighborhood where people denied the importance of differences in order to minimize tension in a very diverse setting. Key demographic characteristics were dismissed as unimportant in a quest for common ground. Instead, respect for individuality and appreciation for each person's ability to contribute were defined as the essentials.

This approach was no doubt of benefit to the neighborhood. And, at first glance, it appears to be a mature approach to diversity. But it had—and has—one major drawback: To use it requires ignoring many of the characteristics by which people define themselves.

Ray's understanding of diversity also discounts the reality of collective mixtures—groups of people who either share or are assumed to share common characteristics. He is, for example, only reluctantly aware of the collective, demographically based workforce diversity mixtures that affect how people are treated in organizations. He rejects the notion that demographic diversity plays a role in workplace dynamics. This reluctance to acknowledge the reality and impact of collective similarities and differences can hinder diversity effectiveness as surely as an overemphasis on demographic differences.

Ray's lack of clarity about the diversity approaches makes him resistant to the notion that he has benefited from inclusion efforts. He views his success as entirely merit-driven and unrelated to such efforts. Yet in any company that seriously addresses inclusion, the numbers always come into play when people of color and women earn promotions. This doesn't negate Ray's qualifications. He is undoubtedly talented. The need for inclusion efforts reflects more on the inadequacies of the company to access talent packaged in "different" people than it does on individual contributors.

His disregard for the impact of demographic diversity can also blind him to the reality that organizations don't necessarily work as well for members of some groups as for others. This disregard may be behind his perception that Anglo Americans are more likely to take advantage of opportunity. This perception could encourage him to blame employees when he finds it difficult to access their talents. He may devote all of his attention to "fixing" them on the assumption that they are the problem. In doing so, he may miss important other factors that are responsible for the difficulties. He may, for example, ignore the possibility that the organization's culture alienates or disempowers the employee. In doing so, he will miss an opportunity to change faulty organizational practices and possibly lose an employee who could have made a contribution.

Is Comfortable With Diversity Tension

Discomfort with conflict of any kind makes it difficult for Ray to tolerate diversity tension. To avoid such tension, he aims for respect across all differences. At first glance, this appears to be extreme openness to diversity. But Ray's is an openness that relies on the ability to disregard unwelcome differences. The openness that the most skilled diversity respondents demonstrate is intertwined with considerable sophistication. These respondents fully acknowledge all differences. But they feel no need to embrace them all. Instead, they make decisions on their acceptability based on their impact on meeting organizational requirements.

Core Diversity Skills

★ *Ability to recognize diversity mixtures.* Ray responds to workforce diversity mixtures by acknowledging the existence of differences but denying their significance. He does not, in truth, think in terms of diversity mixtures. Instead, he thinks of individual differences.

★ *Ability to analyze the mixtures and related tensions.* Because Ray only reluctantly acknowledges significant differences and the tensions they can create, he does not practice this skill. Instead, he minimizes acknowledgment of collective differences to the maximum extent.

◀ *Ability to select an appropriate response*. Ray has fully embraced the assimilation decision, as it relates to his ethnicity, and to complying with his organization's traditions and preferences as well as requirements. Ray's assimilation approach to diversity has required a major reliance on responses that minimize or discount differences. He rejects, for example, the "both/and" explanation that would acknowledge that he both deserved his many promotions and benefited from inclusion efforts. His denial of this and other realities that disturb him could have serious consequences. It could distort his perception of reality in ways that keep him from staying on the cutting edge of what is happening at his company.

Without more clarity around organizational dynamics, he could be disadvantaged. He may find it hard to sustain a quality relationship with his company and is likely to have difficulty managing unassimilated elephant employees as well.

The respect for diversity that Ray advocates is, in essence, the "tolerate" decision—one that calls for superficial interactions with minimal conflict. This too may be ultimately unproductive. Where people must work together for long periods in close contact, respect must mean something more. It must include acknowledgment of genuine differences, including demographic differences, and acceptance and management of the resulting tension.

Ray can enhance his diversity effectiveness considerably by accepting the reality that real differences do exist; some of these differences are more acceptable in an organizational setting than others, and significant differences can be counted on to result in tension.

What's Next for Ray?

Ray has demonstrated considerable flexibility and creativity in forging a successful career for himself in an industry that he once deemed undesirable. His openness to change and willingness to learn have allowed him to see the industry as worthy of an educated person's attention and interesting in its own right.

His creativity has allowed him to combine his desire to teach with his interest in financial matters.

He has created a situation where his personal needs and those of the company appear to be in sync. Ray is a successful elephant in a giraffe house and anticipates that he will continue to be so.

He could strengthen his managerial effectiveness and his ability to continue to grow and advance by engaging diversity more fully and addressing it more directly. This will ensure that he continues to demonstrate the characteristics that have brought him success. It will ensure that the need to manage a workforce increasingly characterized by unassimilated diversity will not exceed his diversity management capabilities as well.

Carol's Story

I'm an Asian American woman in my forties and a marketing director at a business services company. I've been at this company for about ten years. I worked on the East Coast for the first five years. The past five years I've been in the Southwest.

I was with a products-oriented company for fifteen years before coming here. I really enjoyed my first organization. It was an extremely innovative company. In fact, if you were not making something new, you were questioned.

I changed companies because I wanted to work in a more services-marketing-oriented company. I really believe that services marketing is where it's at from a professional standpoint. In addition, I didn't think I had as much potential in my former company. The glass ceiling was pretty low. Certain comments told me I was at a disadvantage. For example, in that culture, you needed to go international to get ahead. I would tell people I wanted to do that. When I did, I got strange looks and questions that bordered on the illegal. They'd ask, for example, "What would your husband do?" I could also see there weren't many women or people of color at the higher levels.

When I first came to this company, I worked in the new products area of the core organization. The work was exciting. But this was the traditional part of the business, and it rewarded certain kinds of behaviors. The general goal was to protect what you have—somewhat defensive.

Since the transfer, I've worked in a start-up group within the organization. It's a totally different world. We have phenomenal growth and huge competitive forces against us. The market environment requires that we be very different from the rest of the company. As a result, we're pretty entrepreneurial, high-growth, and fast-paced. Our business is offensive as well as defensive—a full game.

From the outside looking in, it appears as though we have lots of freedom, and people envy our ability to do our own thing. Still, we do have some constraints. We have a lot of responsibility back to the corporate core, and we have to vie for resources and dollars.

I'm not at the level where I have to fight the huge political battles or arm-wrestle for resources. A lot of my job is getting things to work among cross-functional groups that are both very different and have a lot of interdependencies. I love my work. My career goal is to advance to vice president of marketing and ultimately to a general manager's role.

Individual and Organizational Fit

When I first came to this company, I was pleasantly surprised to find more diversity at the higher levels here than at my former organization. But for some reason, it's not as diverse as it was. Our CEO is a person of color, and there are women at higher levels. And that's wonderful. But there are no Asian Americans at the highest levels. In fact, I'm the highest-ranking Asian American here. It's difficult being the only Asian American at my organizational level in this company. I often feel that the whole weight of the world is on my shoulders.

This company is still good, and I'm still satisfied with my decision to come here. But it could be a better place, particularly in the area of promotions. Results matter. But other things may matter more. Appearances are important, and it sometimes seems as if those who toot their own horn the loudest move up the fastest. That rubs me the wrong way, being Asian and female. It also goes against the idea of teams that my company is advancing.

Assimilation's Ambiguities

I'm a third-generation Japanese American, born and raised in California. My father came from Japan; my mother was American born, of Japanese ancestry. Both spoke English except when they didn't want us to understand. My parents said, "We live in the United States, so we will speak English."

My family was so assimilated that I always thought I was white. In fact, I was termed a banana—yellow on the outside, white on the inside. I was always with Caucasians. I didn't meet many Asian Americans even though I went to public schools. I'm sure there were Asian organizations when I was in college, but I never thought to look for them.

I married a Caucasian, but I kept my name. Something in me knew I needed to do that.

My level of assimilation has been both a blessing and a curse. On the one hand, it allows me to maneuver through the mainstream pretty well, although I still miss some of the subtleties. On the other hand, it creates some dissonance. Sometimes I'll be in a social setting full of Caucasians and catch a glimpse of myself. I'll think, "I look very different from everybody, and this is weird."

I started thinking about my ancestry about five years ago when I realized that things weren't going as well as I had expected. I do a lot of introspection, and I have very high expectations. I would have liked to see myself at a higher level at this point. Why am I not there? Am I not personally qualified or ambitious enough, or is it because I'm a female and looked like a girl well into my thirties or because I'm an Asian American? It gets very blurred.

I don't know how to find out. People within the organization don't volunteer really honest feedback, and it's hard for me to ask, "What's standing in my way?" It would be so helpful to have somebody who can see the situation clearly enough to say, "This is what it is." Everything's so subtle, I can't quite figure it out.

I don't want to walk around with a chip on my shoulder. How do I get through the clutter to get to why?

External Support

One thing that has been very helpful to me is to become active in Asian American organizations. In the early 1990s, I participated in a powerful training program that focused on being an Asian American woman as well as developing leadership skills.

The mentoring and support I get from participating in this and other groups have been more helpful to me than internal mentors have been. Things here move so fast that it's not wise to cling to any one person. If that person leaves the company, the whole situation changes. Even if you have a wonderful mentor who stays, it doesn't guarantee your personal long-term success. It's fascinating, trying to do your job and pay attention to this other stuff.

Participating in Asian American women's groups has done more than provide me with insights into my cultural roots and training in leadership skills. It has resulted in having some of my activities publicized as well.

I enjoy working in a fast-paced environment, working on new things. I like to see results, and I love the business world. I particularly love watching the business grow. I like having competitors because it makes me better. But there is another side of me too. I'm very community-oriented, and I try to find a balance between my work and my desire to give back to my community. I gravitate toward women's issues and, more recently, toward Asian American issues as well.

Last year one of the Asian American organizations had me interviewed by our city's major newspaper as an awardee of one of the communities where I had volunteered my time. The response at work was interesting. People came up to me and said, ``I didn't know you could do that. Why don't you talk more about what you do?''

My general manager came to me and said, ``You're really doing a lot. That's great.'' That might have been one of the little turning points. He had been saying that he was a supporter of mine. But when it came time for promotional opportunities, he didn't act that way. Now something has changed because I'm being told that I'm on different slates of candidates for other jobs. I don't know that that was it, but I feel as if I have more support.

Diversity Defined

To me, diversity within the context of a corporation is where there is a mix. First, I think of gender diversity and people of color. Then

I go to the next level and think in terms of diversity of thinking, style, experience, and personality. These are important in building a team. They are particularly important if your only pool of talent is white men.

In my group we appreciate diversity of personality and style—sometimes, I think, a little too much. We can get into some long-winded discussions that may not accomplish much and make the meetings drag on too long.

I'm becoming more aware of sexual preference and physical ability diversity as well. Another significant mix is diversity of age or experience. In addition, I see a diversity of functional groups, since much of my work is cross-functional.

Experiences With Stereotyping

Within a personal context, diversity has meant something different. Much of my personal experience with diversity has been as a result of having others stereotype me. As a child, I had people telling me I must be very smart because I am Asian American. As an adult, I've had people imply that I am not a minority. "Your people are doctors and scientists and have lots of money," they say. The problem is that a lot of Asian Americans aren't and don't.

Within the business community, I experienced stereotyping first in my former company. For a time during the 1980s, my job required me to drive about 500 miles a week in a rural area. All of my clients were white males. I think a lot of them agreed to meet with me because they were curious about my name, which is very Asian. I would constantly get comments such as, "You speak really good English." "Where are you really from?"

Even within this organization, people see an Asian American woman and pigeonhole me, in spite of what I do. When I go into a meeting, for example, I always say something pertinent and contribute to the conversation because I was told early on that I was too quiet. Yet people still say after the meeting, "You're really quiet." What do I have to do? Hog the entire conversation? I'm learning to say, "You didn't hear what I said." It takes a long time to try to break perceptions.

Sometimes it can be difficult to tell which perceptions spring from stereotyping and which are true to reality. For example, I have been coached that I need to take more risks, and that may be so, given the environment. But I've also been told that I have a very good business head. My dilemma is both to assess the validity of the advice and to figure out how to take sufficient risks and make good business decisions.

Stereotyping happens on a broader level as well. American society lumps all Asians into an Asian/Pacific Islander pigeonhole. For example, people will say to me, "You must speak Chinese." I say, "No, I don't. That's not my ancestry."

It's ironic because the Asian community is very fractured. Koreans, for example, dislike the Japanese people. I've gone into Korean stores and been looked at negatively. My mother feels animosity toward Koreans. She'll say, "I don't want to go to that restaurant. I think it's run by Koreans."

I don't agree with her views, but I also realize that I stereotype too if I'm not careful. Sometimes I'll be in a store and see somebody else who is Asian and think, "I wonder if she has an accent." At other times, I've been on a committee and, based on my first impression, thought, "I don't have much in common with these people," or wondered if they would have much to contribute. I'm always pleasantly amazed that different people have so many talents you don't even know about.

Stereotyping can become discrimination in both organizations and the larger society. Within organizations, discrimination against Asian Americans is subtle. In some corporations, for example, there are a ton of Asian scientists and technical people who are well educated and well paid. But there definitely is a glass or, some say, a bamboo ceiling. Very few of those people are considered for promotion. Most get clustered in the quasi-management/technical bucket—"He really wants to be a scientist."

Within the larger society, we're forgotten and melded in with the mainstream except when it's convenient to set us apart. When people were investigating the political fund-raising irregularities of the 1994 presidential campaign, Asian American donors who had been citizens for years were called and questioned about their donation. The investigators called everybody with a funny last name. They made no distinction between an Asian from Indonesia and a third-generation Asian American.

Yet if Asian Americans complain, others don't understand. Sometimes people look at me and say, "What are you complaining about? You make a lot of money. So what's your beef?"

CAROL AS EFFECTIVE DIVERSITY RESPONDENT

Although Carol has experienced considerable career success, she is concerned that she won't achieve to the level of her aspirations. She struggles to understand the dynamics that have hampered her progress, even though she now expects a breakthrough soon.

Carol's Diversity Maturity

Accepts Responsibility

Carol understands that demographic diversity has implications in her organization. She has accepted responsibility for trying to understand her situation. She has confronted the perception that she is quiet by speaking up and challenging those who ignore her actions, and she has moved out beyond the organization for support.

But she remains reluctant to change some personal behaviors so as to align them with organizational success requirements. She observes, for example, that appearances and tooting your own horn are important, but sees this as inappropriate for her because she is an Asian American and a woman. She also believes that looking "like a girl" blocked her advancement for several years. But she saw little recourse other than to wait to age and appear more mature.

Carol may hesitate to take more direct action on her own behalf because she is uncertain that her perception is clear enough to act on, given the subtlety of others' perceptions and behaviors. Yet she clearly believes that her career has been affected by forces beyond her control—her gender, ethnic background, youthful appearance, and the stereotyping by others—

and she wishes to get past these barriers. She awaits someone who sees clearly and can tell her what to do to achieve her aspirations. Stated differently, she yearns for a mentor and sponsor who can facilitate her advancement.

Carol has not assumed direct responsibility for enhancing the diversity management of her organization. She has, however, taken on broad community-based responsibilities to ensure adequate representation of people with demographically based differences. This is consistent with her current linking of inclusion with diversity.

Demonstrates Contextual Knowledge

Understanding of Self and the Organization. Carol has clear success aspirations. She understands herself and her priorities. She understands her organization's culture and its priorities as well. She is happy with both—with one key exception: She dislikes the success requirements that call for more self-promotion and assertiveness than she is comfortable with. She has found it difficult to assimilate to the requirements in order to achieve her aspirations.

Conceptual Clarity About Diversity. Carol defines diversity first as gender, ethnicity, and race. She sees physical ability as a significant dimension too. She also acknowledges diversity of personality and style. Her cross-functional work allows her to see functional and systems diversity as important as well. In addition, she is very aware of intragroup differences. She relies, for example, on personality and style to distinguish groups comprising all white men.

For Carol, diversity is primarily about inclusion. She seems not to have developed a range of responses for addressing different diversity mixtures. She perceives others as shaping situations, so she appears more focused on their perceptions and thoughts than on how she might leave her mark. This can leave her without a guiding framework for addressing diversity issues.

Is Clear About Requirements

Carol is clear about requirements, but sees some as more legitimate than others. For example, she sees "results" as legitimate, but "other things" or "other stuff" as less significant. In reality, however, all are organizationally legitimate if her managers decide they are. She is free to ignore those requirements that make her uncomfortable, but doing so may have a cost.

Copes With Diversity Complexity and Tension

Carol is uncomfortable around diversity tension. She reports not liking the split that exists among Asian American groups. She also reports that a family value was to fit in—to speak and behave in ways that avoided creating feelings of separation and discomfort. She has successfully done this. In addition, her concern for and interest in community predisposes her to prefer and seek out situations that promote harmony and minimize intergroup or interpersonal tensions.

Yet her coworker's admonition that she should take more risks may be applicable here. She must be willing to endure and get past diversity tension if she is to express herself adequately and, in the process, impress those with the power to further her career.

Places Differences in Context

Carol's personal experiences with being stereotyped have made it difficult for her to place differences in context. Ironically, her participation in culture-specific programs may make this more challenging as well.

This attribute of diversity maturity requires letting go of stereotypes—those that apply to ourselves as well as to others. Carol's perception of being stereotyped has left her very aware of how others see Asian Americans. Her experiences in the culture-specific programs have sensitized her to culture-specific propensities and their implications. She gives some evidence of having bought into cultural stereotypes regarding both women and Asian Americans and applying them to herself. She concludes, for example, that being a woman and an Asian-American makes it difficult for her to toot her own horn.

In addition, neither experience has prepared her to assess differences—her own or those of others—based on their implications within a specific context. Nor have they prepared her to have her differences assessed based on this criterion. They have encouraged her instead to think of differences per se rather than differences and their impact within a given setting.

The placement and evaluation of differences within a specific context would make a major contribution to Carol's diversity maturity.

Core Diversity Skills

Ability to recognize diversity mixtures. Carol routinely identifies several diversity mixtures. She speaks at length of ethnic diversity and stereotyping and their implications on her life.

Ability to analyze the mixtures and related tensions. Her intuitive response to the tensions associated with this mix has been to assimilate, which she notes has had some definite advantages. Her response to others' differences, however, appears to be more varied. She notes that the expression of personality and stylistic differences among her employees may take an inordinate amount of time. But she appears ready to see that this happens. Still, she seems not to have thought to assess differences based on their impact on the ability to meet organizational requirements. This seems, in part at least, to reflect her belief in the inherent value of inclusion.

Ability to select an appropriate response. Her response to the ethnicity mix at this point appears on the face to rely heavily on stereotyping, particularly as it concerns her personal ancestry. She both stereotypes herself and focuses on how others have stereotyped her.

It is likely that the first has a very practical purpose. She may be reclaiming her ancestry so as to achieve an appropriate balance. She will no doubt continue to assimilate in numerous situations while expressing her ethnicity when this is appropriate. Her focus on others' stereotyping may have a negative effect on her career advancement. To define a problem as the consequence of the perceptions and behaviors of others is to relinquish the ability to solve it. She may benefit from minimizing stereotyping as the reason for any career-related disappointments and framing the issues in ways that leave her opportunities to find solutions.

Carol operates within the context of the requirements mix as well. She does not identify this as a diversity issue. But she is nonetheless aware of the dynamics.

She sees two kinds of requirements: those related to work and performance and those referred to as "other things" or "other stuff." She assimilates readily to those related to work and performance. She does not fully embrace those she associates with the "other stuff." Instead, she tolerates them. In fact, she sees herself as not suited to satisfy some key requirements in this category and seems not to be convinced that it is appropriate to require them. She does not anticipate, for example, tooting her own horn.

Yet she is becoming more aware of the significance of not meeting those requirements that she perceives as secondary. And her recent responses and changing perceptions suggest that she is on the verge of adopting a "foster mutual adaptation" response. Taking advantage of external support and advocacy, for example, satisfies the need to stand out in order to achieve recognition without violating her sense of who she is and how she wants to behave.

Carol does not report on her responses to other diversity mixtures. But her interview and values suggest that they are likely to revolve around responses that minimize diversity: suppression, denial, and assimilation. It is likely that around these mixes, as around the ethnicity mix, she will benefit from stepping out, achieving more comfort with diversity tension and choosing, when appropriate, response options that maximize rather than minimize diversity.

WHAT'S NEXT FOR CAROL?

Carol's choice of a work environment that is entrepreneurial, high-growth, and fast-paced indicates that she enjoys meeting and mastering a challenge. Her results-oriented stance suggests that she will most likely move toward more varied and flexible responses to diversity as she experiences the business necessity to do so.

She is currently in transition, from nearly total reliance on assimilation to experiencing a renewed appreciation of her roots. Most recently, she implemented a foster mutual adaptation solution where she met organizational requirements to stand out yet maintained her own stance toward tooting her own horn by having an outside organization publicize her achievements.

The degree to which she learns to appreciate and demonstrate all of the diversity options when appropriate will help determine how others see her. This may well have implications for her continued advancement. She has little to lose by taking some risks.

7

The Angry Elephants:
Debra and Mark

Debra's Story

I am a black woman in my late thirties. I've been with this consumer products organization for fourteen years. For the first
twelve or so years, I progressed regularly in my career development. Then about eighteen months ago, the organization went
through a major reduction in force. People were realigned and
responsibilities reassigned.

It was a terrible experience. I was retained. But it was scary.
They didn't assign me to a new position right away. They let one
regional marketing person go, and the other retired early, so I
was left to take care of the food business for the entire company.
I didn't learn until May 1997 what my new assignment was. They
took me off the food business, which didn't make sense since no
one else in the company understood the business, and put me
on the West Team. I've been there ever since.

The New Order

The West Team comprises a team leader, a marketing person, an
administrative assistant, and two sales managers—a black male
who has sales experience but lacks experience in the company
and the business, and myself. We're supposed to work according
to a "team process."

The team leader is a woman I used to work with. Although

she is technically not my manager, she acts if she is. This woman has only limited managing experience. She had supervised first-level salespeople and doesn't know how to manage more experienced and senior people. In my career, every time I've gotten a non-manager-trained manager, I've had problems.

The marketing person, who had no sales experience, took on a sales role during my absence. She approaches customers from a perspective very different from mine. These two white women established a bond and a system during the eight months they worked together before I came on board. I'm not privy to either. To make matters worse, I picked up a territory that was not originally a part of the team's responsibility, so the team leader has no knowledge of the account base of this geographical area.

I'm not comfortable with the team or the new system, and I guess it shows. My team leader has complained that I don't communicate with the team. I admit it is difficult for me to call somebody and ask for input. I'm used to making decisions on a regional level, and I know the system. I think I'm contributing because I'm not pulling on her time.

This person has been on only one account call with me in a year and a half, so she really doesn't know how I operate. I feel that there's an undercurrent—a lot of little subtleties—and I don't know what that is. I've asked her to be direct because I can't read minds, and I can't correct something if I don't know what that something is. I don't know how to deal with the situation, and I'm at a point in my life where I don't know if I want to deal with it.

I'm not comfortable with this new organization either. We're moving to different selling styles. We were bought by another company. I have no idea what the new company's strategies are or what its culture is like. There has been a lot of change and uncertainty over the past two years. Long-term, high-level people have been let go or demoted. I think the organization is about to explode—in either a very positive or very negative way.

This past year has been the most traumatic year of my career and the least productive for me as a person and as a professional. I really am burned out in trying to define who I am, what my strengths and weaknesses are, and what an asset I may or may not be to the company. That's been a big issue for me. I'm not sure who I want to be. I know a change needs to happen. I don't know if it will happen with this company, or if I need to leave the industry or work within the industry at another company.

An Earlier Reassessment

I had one other period when I felt the need to reassess what I was doing. My mother died when I was twenty-five. My mother was a beautician. She was a very gregarious woman and a workaholic, and she had a highly successful business. She was also my best friend and my idol. She taught me how to be a social being, how to manage money, and how to manipulate in my environment. I grew up wanting to be like her.

Before she died, she made me promise I would not follow in her footsteps and be a workaholic. At the time she died, I was working eighty or ninety hours a week. I had no social life outside of church.

Her death made me reassess what was really important. I realized that there should be a balance in life. You can get a lot of fulfillment out of a career, but there are other things. Before her death, I had never seen myself as someone's wife or mother. When she died, I reconsidered. I realized I needed a certain amount of challenge, but I didn't need to work ninety hours a week to get that. I began to work less even though it meant a pay cut. Five years later, I married and had children.

Being in Charge

I'm used to taking charge of my life. Very early in my career, I had a difficult time with a first-line manager. He was telling others things about me that weren't true and could have cost me my image and my job. I solved it by going over his head. I wasn't going down without a fight.

My encounter with this manager shook me up. I had never had an adversary in the workforce. It made me very protective of how I am perceived. It also taught me not to trust anybody else with my career development. I take full responsibility for that. If I have to go over my manager's head, I'll do that.

In the past, I've taken charge of my destiny here as well. I've always challenged myself as a person and a professional. I've been able to work out of my home when I'm not traveling. I could never function in an environment where I had to punch in. I got that characteristic from my grandmother. She had a thriving neighborhood general store. She just refused to work for white people. This woman, who had a third-grade education, put six kids through school.

To preserve that freedom, I set higher standards for myself than the company ever set. The long hours and hard work are a trade-off for the ability to work independently and make a comfortable living.

The Value of a Mentor

Still, my way of doing things has its drawbacks. A few years ago I realized that the really successful people in this organization are the white males who golf and are very strong politicians, those who are very good at schmoozing. I watched how they played and worked, and compared it with the amount of work I did, and I realized that something was terribly wrong. A light bulb went off. I realized how important relationships were.

I thought, "I understand about hard work and profits, but I don't understand how to work the system. I'm so volume-driven that I'm not necessarily working on polishing up the persona in order to move to the next position. I'm not good at the mechanics of selling me. I need someone who has the power and the willingness to speak for me internally. In short, I need a mentor."

Usually mentors seek you out. Instead, I went to them. I was very direct. I said, "I need a mentor. I don't understand how to work the system, and I am not strong in the internal politics. I need help. Train me."

I asked one woman and one man. Both were third-level managers, one in marketing and the other in sales. Both agreed, although the man took a little selling. These mentors helped me a great deal. They made sure my strengths and accomplishments were known by the decision makers. They presented me in a light that made it possible for me to be a regional manager. They affected my income and provided enormous support. They also provided a sounding board and a safe environment. They identified areas where I needed to improve and helped me work those issues out.

Both of my mentors are gone. When we went through the reduction in force, a lot of people left and a lot of others were let go. I could use them now.

Conflicts

My team leader and I have already had several conflicts, most of which I don't understand. She obviously does not trust me. Not long ago I found out secondhand that she had asked the marketing person from our team to attend a fact-finding meeting with a new client, without even mentioning it to me, although all the sales and marketing managers were told. No one from our company had ever approached this client; then, when I did, it was as if they wanted to take the account over. At other times, I'm made important contributions. But neither she nor other team members have given me credit for them.

Sources of Tension

Several things may be contributing to the situation. On the one hand, it seems as if race is an issue. I'm not sure she's comfortable with me as a black person, much less one who—how can I say this?—there's not much I feel she can teach me. She's not had to work with any blacks in the company. Hank is the only other black person on the team, and he's a totally different issue. He's chronologically much younger, and he's a baby in the company. So he's not going to approach the business the same way that I do.

Still, race isn't our only difference. I don't have much respect for her management capabilities. Before the reorganization, she was a district manager and was responsible for first-level salespeople. In managing brokers, I had to work with presidents and owners, as well as accounts people. I have had to adapt to my subordinates' needs to get the best out of them. My management style is to hold everyone accountable for meeting requirements but to treat people differently, based on where and who they are. I've had other managers do that for me as well.

I expect my team leader to do this for me too. It's just not happening. Maybe I'm getting too old to change, or maybe I'm too rigid. But it bothers me that she thinks she can manage me like she manages someone who has been only six months on the job and that she doesn't recognize that I have other levels of contribution.

It also bothers me that she expects me to share information about my personal life. My personal life I share only to a degree. My professional life, we can get very much into details. But the two don't marry. I've told my team members this. But it appears to create friction, particularly with my team leader.

I don't think my team leader communicates. She never clarifies requirements. From her perspective, I know what she wants. Her point, as I understand it, is that *I'm* not communicative; therefore, we are not communicating. It's becoming a real problem. If we don't sort the relationship out, she'll be a stumbling block for me. In fact, I'm already hearing things that make me wonder what she's sharing with others.

Helping Newer Minorities Along

It has always been challenging to be a black female in this organization. When I look at the company, I see a pecking order. I see black males and white females at the same level under the white males. When it comes to ethnicity, Caucasians are still at the top; people of non-African descent fall into line. They are perceived very differently from people of African descent. We're at the bottom.

Because I'm a black female who grew up in the South, I've had to prove myself over and over. Still, I had the naive notion that after some point, I would be judged on my own history and merit. It's not true. Maybe other races view it the same way in corporate America, but I find it an obvious requirement for blacks.

Recently the company hired six blacks—most of whom had never been in the field. Of the six, five are women. The most recent is the second salesperson on my team.

Most of what I know about the company, blacks taught me—not my white counterparts or managers. To see a whole group of people as unwilling or unable to help is unproductive. So I try to share with these newcomers how to work the system and help them become aware of the pitfalls. I try to direct them to resources that can help them accomplish what they need to, because if you don't know, you just don't know. That's what people did for me when I came into the organization. I try to warn and share with other blacks and tell them that if they hear something I need to know to call me at home. The last thing I want is to be blindsided.

All but the salesperson on my team are receptive to this. They call and run things past me. I tried that with my teammate, but I'm very guarded with him because he just married a white female. My impression is that he thinks that because he married this woman, whites will embrace him. He is very guarded with me. He seems to think he might end up in the middle of this thing between my team leader and me.

Still, I'd like to help him. In some meetings my team leader and marketing person have questioned this man's achievements, and I can tell they're not comfortable with his interracial marriage. I've offered to manage him on certain accounts and tried to tell him these things in very subtle ways. I told him that he should be guarded about what he shares of his personal life. I've also told him what he needed to do and how to get there. I told him, ``I'll share with you what I know. When I don't know, I will direct you to other people who do know. These people will give you an honest response. In addition, it's safe to ask them the questions. That's important because you can't trust everybody in the organization.''

Looking to the Future

Change usually doesn't bother me, but this change has been so fierce that I find it draining. I'm tired of having to deal with managers who don't know how to manage. I'm tired of having to prove myself all over again because this person cannot value diversity. I've tried to tell her, ``I don't have to approach the business like you do. I just have to meet requirements.''

At this point in my life I have accumulated stuff. Now I'm wondering, ''Is this stuff worth having? Will I automatically lose it if I change career courses, or can I maintain it doing something that's more beneficial to myself? If I lose it, will I survive?'' I'm in the process of evaluating everything.

To look at this in a positive light, if you don't have friction, you don't have growth. It's important that I stay focused on handling the stress of that. At some point I'm going to move past this.

DEBRA AS EFFECTIVE DIVERSITY RESPONDENT

Clearly Debra's work environment is stressful. The unexpected acquisition of her company and subsequent reduction in force left her with a long period of uncertainty and, ultimately, with a new position where she is uncomfortable and feels unvalued. Along with this, she lost her mentors, people who had supported her and advocated for her success. This blow in itself would have been enough to leave her reeling.

Debra also experiences her reduced organizational status vividly. She notes her difficulty with working under a non-manager-trained manager and the stress and relative lack of rewards associated with working with nonstrategic accounts.

Debra's continued discomfort and considerable anger about her changed organization and status partly reflect circumstances beyond her control. But they reflect her current lack of motivation and subsequent inability to address workforce diversity effectively as well. Debra has become entrenched in a response pattern characterized by increasing isolation and defensiveness. When she must interact with her team manager, she responds with toleration. She is correct in noting that changes are needed.

Debra's Diversity Maturity

Accepts Responsibility

Debra reports that in the past, she assumed responsibility for interacting successfully with a diverse group of brokers and employees. Indeed, she considers herself to be highly skilled at managing employees with diverse needs and criticizes her team leader's inadequacy in this area.

At present, her anger prevents her from examining her own role in her unsatisfactory relationship with her team leader and other members. Instead she focuses on the inscrutability of the organization and the difficulty of getting along with her cohorts. Debra feels so disconnected from her organization that she focuses on what's wrong with it without speculating on how she could improve its functioning, let alone its diversity effectiveness. Her quest for relief has muted broader concerns. This is unfortunate because enhanced diversity management effectiveness would go a long way toward ameliorating her situation.

Demonstrates Contextual Knowledge

An Understanding of the Organization. Before the acquisition, Debra appears to have understood the organization and to have worked out a way to meet both the organization's and her own requirements. Now, however, she cannot. She reports ongoing frustration at her inability to understand the organization's goals and strategies.

Mission and Vision. Debra reports that before the acquisition she was very clear about her personal mission and vision, as well as about her organization's priorities. Much of her current discomfort stems from her uncertainty about these basics and the necessity of refining or redefining them on both a personal and organizational basis. She will undoubtedly be on much firmer ground once she does this.

Conceptual Clarity About Diversity. Debra's reports of her past management efforts indicate that she was accustomed to defining diversity broadly and managing it effectively, particularly in relationships with subordinates. Her relationships with her managers indicate that she was less likely to see tensions with them as resolvable through face-to-face negotiations and more likely to go around these individuals than to craft mutual adaptation solutions with them.

Although she undoubtedly retains her knowledge of the

breadth of diversity dimensions, she is currently focusing on only a few and emphasizing differences to the exclusion of similarities. As a result of her stress and distress, she is neglecting to use her diversity insights to her own and her organization's best advantage.

Is Clear About Requirements

Debra clearly understands the concept of requirements as they relate to productivity-related issues: "You need to define for me what the requirement is," she tells her team leader. Yet she is ignoring a significant newly defined requirement: harmonious relationships and interdependence among team members. She is instead acting out of her strong preference to avoid contact to the extent possible. In doing so, she is diminishing her opportunity to meet her own requirements—the ability to maintain maximum independence while remaining a valued part of the organization.

Since she reports—and the evidence indicates—that she grounded her past decisions on requirements, her current behavior most likely stems from unhappiness about and anger at the situation rather than confusion about the concept.

Debra indicates that she is revisiting her own requirements. Her past behavior indicates that should she become convinced that her current behavior isn't helping to meet her requirements, she will change her behavior. Her willingness to reflect on her requirements and behaviors and to bring them into sync when necessary are critical traits for effective diversity respondents.

Is Comfortable With Diversity Tension

Although Debra sees herself as direct, even confrontational, in truth, she appears very uncomfortable with diversity tension. Consistently her solution to such tension is to use a variety of techniques that allow her to keep her distance. She operates in an us-them mode when interacting with new African American employees. She circumvented the manager she felt was working against her. She resists friendly as well as nonfriendly gestures on the part of her team leader and members. She is less likely to confront diversity tension than to avoid it.

Core Diversity Skills

🖎 *Ability to identify diversity mixtures.* Debra identifies style as a significant diversity mix. She reports that in three critical areas—directness, decision making, and intimacy—her style and that of her team leader and members diverge. In doing so, she places herself within the diversity mix and assigns to herself part of the responsibility for the ongoing tensions. Debra reports that she prefers a direct and confrontational style; her team leader does not. (Her interview, however, suggests that this may be more perception than reality.) The team leader prefers a collegial participatory decision-making style. Debra finds this intrusive. She interprets the team leader's insistence on being involved as evidence of a lack of trust. Finally, the team leader prefers sharing personal issues; Debra dislikes such sharing. To date, she has chosen to tolerate her team leader when compelled to interact with her.

Debra recognizes—indeed emphasizes—the race mixture. Here, however, she has more difficulty accepting responsibility for her role in the interactions that accompany this mix. She is aware, for example, that her team leader appears uncomfortable about race, but seems not to notice the full impact of her own discomfort with this mix.

Debra may be correct in believing that race is a factor in the ongoing tension, but she must be careful. There are obviously other important mixtures. If her awareness of race obscures other mixtures and tensions, she will be left with a distorted view and a thwarted career within her company. If her distrust of this mixture causes her to behave in ways that intimidate or concern her team leader and members, her emphasis on the race mixture will become a liability.

🖎 *Ability to analyze the mixtures and related tensions.* Debra provides evidence that at one time she routinely analyzed diversity mixtures and tensions and used this information to manage others. Currently she does not. Her sense that she is in survival mode has left her unable to broaden her perspective and determine what impact the mixture and tension have on her ability to meet organizational requirements.

🖋 *Ability to select an appropriate response.* Debra has been unable to emulate her grandmother's actions by refusing to work for whites. But she has remained true in spirit. She works for but only tolerates white people, keeping her interactions with them superficial. Her team leader invites collaboration; Debra refuses the invitation. Her coworker discusses family happenings; Debra replies in noncommittal ways.

Before the acquisition of her company, Debra had achieved a balance between her preference for independence and distrust of racial integration, and her company's systems and requirements. She had taken the initiative in finding sponsors and had crafted a mutually beneficial relationship that allowed her to succeed in spite of her particular requirements. In the highly individualistic culture of the organization's past, Debra's choice of toleration had fewer career consequences. She was good at her job, and her mentors helped her with the relationship aspects of her career.

The acquisition of her company changed all that. Debra is now an unassimilated elephant. Her preference for independence puts her at odds with the evolving team orientation. Her style differs from that of her team leader and other members. And her distrust of racial mixtures and her company has come to the fore.

Debra's "tolerate" choice may leave her at a disadvantage. She reports confusion about the new company's strategies and finds its culture incomprehensible, thus defining herself as an outsider. Yet she is in the midst of a team that is demonstrating the new agenda. This is particularly unfortunate because she reports that she thrived when she asked for and received mentor support. Her current stance makes it unlikely that she will receive such assistance.

Debra must reexamine her choice of action options. Ultimately she will benefit from choosing once again the option of fostering mutual adaptation. It suits her focused and action-oriented style and puts the emphasis on meeting organizational objectives. She will benefit professionally from agreeing to assimilate sufficiently to ensure continued success while maintaining most of those qualities by which she defines herself. She will undoubtedly experience pain, however, in going against the message she received from her grandmother. Her assimilation decision won't come easily.

What's Next for Debra?

Debra's next moves depend on three things: the conclusions she reaches as a result of her current reassessment, her ability or inability to make peace with her grandmother's admonition, and her ability to keep her distrust from becoming dysfunctional.

Debra's reassessment process covers a large number of variables: age, frustration, value to the company, choice of a company, and broader hopes for the future. Several things could happen. She may conclude that her requirements can be met with the company, seek out a mutual adaptation solution with her team manager and other members, and work toward understanding the company. She may conclude that she and the company are not a good fit and leave. Or she may remain on the fence, staying with the company but remaining distrustful and making insufficient change to ensure that it is a productive experience.

Whatever the decision, Debra will benefit from crafting a resolution that leaves her less angry and distrustful, thus allowing her to reassert and hone her earlier demonstrated potential as an effective diversity respondent.

Mark's Story

I am an African American man in my early thirties and a sales rep for a food industry company. I joined this organization after six years in product development and two years as a sales representative with another consumer products company. I left when I was told I should expect to stay with the company ten years before I moved up.

The organization I work for is entrepreneurial and relatively young. It has grown at an extraordinary rate for each of the past fifteen years, and has gone from 100 to 2,000 reps during this time. It's an exciting place to work. I thrive in situations where I'm given autonomy, and this organization does that. People are cordial and civil and treat each other with respect, at least in day-to-day work. It's an aggressive company. Senior management wants to know that everyone they hire can be motivated by money. Managers go out of their way to see that employees are happy and want to stay, and there are lots of opportunities because of the growth.

I'm pretty aggressive myself. I'm also driven, self-disciplined, analytical, an achiever, and a team player if necessary. I get along with everybody. I just finished my M.B.A. in international marketing. At some point, I plan to run a company.

I joined this company for the opportunity to go into sales with an uncapped bonus potential. I came under the impression that because I possessed previous sales experience, if I proved myself in sales, I would move along quickly. I've been here three years, and I'm still a sales rep. My first year, I was in the top 10 percent of the sales force. In the next twelve months, I was in the top 5 percent. Last year I got an award for being consistent and a team player. My longer-term goal is to go into team management. My intermediate goal is to go into the marketing department. Since most of the marketing department comes directly from sales, this is a natural transition.

Disillusionment

Until recently I thought this company and I were a good fit. Now I'm not so sure. Last year I was passed over for a promotion. That was the most intense career experience I've had. In fact, I feel so strongly about it that I've been debating whether to quit.

The person who got the promotion came here the same day that I did. I'm much more qualified than she is. I have eight years of product development and sales experience, four years of managerial experience, an M.B.A., the sales accolades, and all that. She came with a lot less experience. Everything she knows about the food industry she learned here. I've outranked her since we came.

Even more infuriating than losing the promotion was the reason I was passed over. I've asked every manager involved to name one area where her qualifications exceed mine. They couldn't identify any. What they said, in effect, is that she got the promotion because she had better relationships. My regional manager told me, ''Once you get to the interview, it's already assumed you have the qualifications. After that, gut feelings and intuition take over.'' The hiring manager told me I need to ''raise the comfort level of the marketing department.''

Responding to the Challenge

I had some early warning that this was going to happen. When I first told my managers I intended to apply for the job, they told me she would be tough competition. She ''had baby-sat for the hiring manager's children and was like family with him.'' Still, I couldn't believe that qualifications wouldn't count more than friendship.

I asked my district manager boss (who was also hers) for support. Your district manager is supposed to sponsor you to the hiring managers when it's time for you to be promoted. Mine stayed on the fence. Next I talked to the regional manager, who played hot potato and threw it back to my boss.

When I realized what was happening, I called the human resources vice president and asked what I should do. He wasn't very encouraging. All he could suggest was to focus on myself and do my best in the interview. So I put together a seventy-five-page document that included a business plan and my résumé and reference letters.

I also called on the marketing vice president. He and I had talked at dinner, and he had asked to accompany me on a sales call one time. I told him the situation. During our conversation, he said, speaking of someone else, ''He did an exceptional job, but he was a nerdy kind of guy. When you hire somebody for marketing, you want to hire somebody you can go out and have a beer with.'' I'm sure my mouth fell open because he quickly said, ''You know I feel comfortable going out and having a beer with you.''

Later, he said, "You know, sometimes it takes people six or more times to get into marketing."

At that point I knew the decision had already been made. This was reconfirmed when the hiring manager said, "You know, when you're hiring, you have to look at the total group and see who is the best fit for the group." When he said that, I knew that that would be the reason I didn't get the job. Sure enough, he sent me a voice prompt saying, "We didn't give you the job because we want the best fit."

In the Aftermath

I asked various managers, "What does 'fit for the group' mean?" "How do you quantify that?" "What were the criteria for the position?" "How did I measure up on those criteria?" "What was I lacking in qualifications?" All of their answers had to do with relationship and fit and intuition and gut feeling or raising the comfort level. The marketing vice president suggested that I talk to people at the national sales meeting.

I was furious about not getting the position. But I knew I couldn't say that to my managers because there would be horrific political consequences. So I talked to the human resources vice president. His only explanation was that African Americans always get passed over the first time they go up for a job that they should get. You end up getting the job the second time. My response was, "That's not acceptable." He said, "It's a matter of time." I said, "We have only have a limited time on this earth, and I don't want to waste my time because they can't figure out how to treat people objectively. I'm out of here. I'm already interviewing."

Help From Higher Up

Things didn't change until the northern sales director came into town and asked to accompany me on a call. As we drove there, he asked me how things were going. I told him about my wife, my three kids. I also told him about the promotion pursuit and the feedback I had gotten. He wasn't very happy. His face was red. He wrote people's names down and told me point-blank, "I'm

gonna call these people because I'm not happy with this."
Shortly after that, my manager experienced a 180-degree turnaround in attitude. Earlier he had said I couldn't spend time in
the marketing department working on a project. Now he encouraged me to do so.

The district manager developed a turbo-charged interest in
my career too. He sent me to a career development seminar,
which was very good. It was interesting because the only people
there were women, three Hispanic males, one Indian man, and
myself. We were obviously a select group.

The hiring manager began calling me for nonsensical reasons. I started hearing from other people in marketing that he
"thinks highly" of me.

During the recent national sales meeting, the hiring manager
called me out of a session to tell me the position I didn't get in
Atlanta was available in Cincinnati. I told him, "Thanks, but no
thanks. Cincinnati is not the power base of the company. I want
to remain in New England or go to Atlanta."

I'm interviewing now for a job that's a step above the promotion I didn't get. I'm being told from all corners of the earth,
"We're going to give you something. You just need to wait twelve
months or so." However, people who may not be privy to the
whole situation have also told me that I shouldn't count on getting the job. Apparently it's tradition for someone to have had a
promotion before getting the kind of marketing position I'm interviewing for now. I'm getting the impression that there was a top-
down decision to make it right, and they're going to give me a
turbo-promotion. Still, that remains to be seen. I haven't seen an
offer on the table.

Thinking Things Through

I'm pleased about this—or at least I will be if I get a promotion.
But unfortunately I could never have the amount of loyalty that I
once had for the organization, because I feel as though I was
misled, misinformed. Clearly there are two kinds of success in this
organization. The first is what they say is success; the second is
what they reward. They define success as performance. For that

they give you money and trips and awards. But to get a reward in the form of a promotion requires stellar relationships.

Within a year and a half after coming here, I had already demonstrated performance. If I had known a year ago that I was outside of the social-political norms—or whatever the case may be—I would have worked on that instead of beating my brains out chasing after performance. I would have spent at least 20 to 30 percent of my field sales time talking to people at the company, building my network. If I had done that, in all likelihood I would have had the job.

I've known that socializing is important. I've been encouraged to have people ride with me in the field, and I've done that. My boss has also encouraged me to call senior managers whom I know just to say, "I like this sales aid," or anything else just so they hear my voice and know my name.

I think that would be a waste of their time and mine. Besides, as an African American male, I don't have room for error. If I call a senior executive about something dumb, I'm going to confirm his perception that we're not too bright. So I feel compelled to contact them with something semi-intelligent.

However, it turns out that after the first year, when you are expected to produce, they expect you to spend 30 to 40 percent of your time developing relationships within the organization. What's more, we define relationships differently. If we're working toward a common business objective, I'm happy to build a relationship with you based on meeting our joint objective.

Their definition is different. It's purely social. Furthermore, when they say *social*, they mean "like family." They even expect people to spend the night at other people's houses. I don't see myself fitting into that scenario. No one would expect to spend the night at my house nor would I expect to spend the night at theirs. They're just not as comfortable with me as they are with the others. I will never be able to achieve the level of comfort of my white counterparts, who have gone to the same schools and played golf with each other.

The reality is that if I were to invite one of the white senior managers to spend the night at my house, he would say, "Oh no, don't trouble yourself." But if one of their white counterparts—someone they play golf with at the national sales meeting—were to invite them, they'd be more likely to say okay. When it comes time for the interview, who is going to get the job: the person the hiring manager has spent the night with—the one whose wife and kids he knows—or me? I'm discouraged.

I know that it would be different if this were a black-owned organization. Then I'd be on equal footing. I know that I could fit in socially. I also know that I can better trust a black person not to assume that I am incompetent, and I can trust a black person to be straight with me more than I can trust a white person.

Passing the Word On

I've been spreading what I've learned to the new African Americans coming into the company. I tell them, "Your first year, it's critical to put out some good numbers. You have to prove performance. But after you've done that, start redistributing your time. Develop a target list of people within the organization who can move you along, just like you do with outside contacts. Create a call record book for them; get to know their personal interests; treat them as you would a customer. Call on them as if it were a sales call. Do this every month so that at a bare minimum they will know exactly who you are, what you're about, what you're trying to do. You don't necessarily have to love these people. But you do have to develop a relationship with them because you have certain business objectives that you want to meet.

Addressing the Larger Problem

I have to admit, though, that even that may not be enough. African Americans have a lot of issues that need to be addressed in managing the social aspect of the job. We don't even have the same definitions as white people do to start. Once we get the definitions correct, the issue becomes how I as a black person in a white society and a white company overcome the baggage that's attached—the presumption of incompetence and the resistance of white people to have close social relationships with black people.

How do I deal with the inevitable conflicts? My white counterparts are allowed to have disagreements with their boss. Typically African Americans cannot do that because then the friction builds. We need to know how to negotiate that relationship with white people and not get them frazzled or uncomfortable. We need to know how to put them at ease quickly and create an atmosphere of mutual confidence. These things just do not happen naturally.

At the very least, I need to learn how to keep the social aspect from being a negative for me. In fact, I've thought about asking if there are any courses I could take to help me get along socially with white people without becoming an Uncle Tom. I'm not talking about assimilation. As far as that's concerned, I've gone as far as I can go. I haven't become "family" yet. But that's the whole question. How does a black person become like family within a white organization? Lacking that, how do I at least reach a point in an organization where the social aspect no longer inhibits my career success?

MARK AS EFFECTIVE DIVERSITY RESPONDENT

Mark's trust in his organization has been shattered by his experiences in seeking a promotion. He is doubly upset because until his experience with his hoped-for promotion, he believed that he and his company enjoyed a good individual-organizational fit. Now he is not sure that he is in the right company, or that he ever can do what is required for managerial upward mobility. This is especially troublesome for him, given that he is without question a high-performing salesperson.

Mark shares with effective diversity respondents an awareness of and willingness to work toward meeting both his own and his organization's objectives. However, he has not connected an ability to address diversity effectively with success in doing so. He has yet to start his diversity journey.

Mark's Diversity Maturity

Accepts Responsibility

Mark appears to have believed that the results-driven culture of his organization would make it unnecessary to manage diversity. He focused on his considerable sales abilities, assuming that other aspects of his career would fall into place. When disillusioned, he challenged his managers' decisions and looked for them to make it right.

Currently, he is asking, in effect, "How can I change enough to appease those who prefer their managers to be like family?" But he has yet to ask, "How can I improve my diversity management skills and help my organization to do the same?" He has not accepted that responsibility. He continues to stand back and wait for his managers to get right on diversity.

Demonstrates Contextual Knowledge

Mission and Vision. Mark understands his company's priorities and strategies. However, he has forgotten to operate out of this understanding when communicating with his managers. In defining diversity within the context of fairness, he has communicated that differences are something to be on guard about, thus weakening his case. He could achieve greater influence and organizational success by focusing on the way in which properly managed diversity could allow his company to strengthen its bottom line.

Conceptual Clarity About Diversity. Because Mark equates diversity with race, he has not sought out the broad understanding of diversity that would allow him to place himself and his situation in perspective or to use diversity concepts as a tool to improving his productivity and effectiveness. He can enhance his diversity maturity by differentiating between inclusion and genuine diversity and by including himself in the diversity mix. He, like his white managers, is a full player, one capable of influencing the results of their interactions.

Is Comfortable With Diversity Tension

Mark's response to the racial diversity tension has been to focus on what others did wrong, to challenge them on their behaviors, and to withdraw emotionally. He has, in fact, "played the race card"—that is, attributed his treatment to the fact that he was black. At issue isn't whether this card is appropriate at times. It is whether using the card at a specific time in a specific situation improves the ability to reach one's objectives. Mark is hopeful that it will.

It is possible, however, that in an organization that values relationships, an approach that accepted responsibility for not internalizing the relationship requirement and a request for coaching and advocacy would have been more effective. Only time will tell. What is evident is that Mark could improve his diversity management skills by routinely seeing diversity tension as the product of the interaction between people who have significant differences, not solely as the result of others' actions.

Core Diversity Skills

🐘 *Ability to identify diversity mixtures.* Mark is experiencing a crisis because his drive to succeed and belief that sales should ensure managerial success as well as financial reward caused him to disregard one significant diversity mixture. His unhappiness with the results is causing him to overemphasize another.

🐘 *Ability to analyze the mixtures and related tensions.* Mark is dealing with a diversity mixture comprising the organizational requirements for financial rewards and those for promotion. Mark hadn't known of this mixture. He had assumed that behaviors that garnered financial rewards would ensure his advancement in the company as well. He is outraged at being passed over for the promotion.

His situation is made more difficult because he doesn't see that it grows out of an inadequately addressed diversity mixture. Yet as he looks back, he realizes that he was, in fact, coached to develop relationships with those who had the power to help him. This and his peers' awareness of the requirement indicate that the requirements mixture was out in the open.

Three factors may have led him to deny or disregard the mixture: his belief that he shouldn't have to address it, his focus on race as the only significant diversity mixture, and his subsequent concern that he would be unable to satisfy the relationship requirement.

When Mark says *diversity*, he means racial differences. He sees these differences as significant enough to prevent him from achieving his goals in a white-owned and -managed organization.

He assumes, for example, that whites are more comfortable with the company's relationship requirements and have greater ability to meet them. He states that whites and blacks define *relationship* differently. Whites, he asserts, are more interested in workplace intimacy, whereas blacks prefer a more business-oriented relationship. He believes that this definition gives whites an edge because African Americans cannot hope to become "like family" in a white-owned company. Racism prevents this from happening.

This may be part of the story. The snapshot nature of his story prevents us from knowing. Still, there is more. In truth, some—perhaps most—whites are no more likely to prefer intimate workplace relationships than are blacks. They, too, would find this requirement threatening.

In addition, Mark indicates that all employees are evaluated based on subjective criteria. He also indicates that employees are expected to pay their dues in ways that would leave many, regardless of demographic characteristics, feeling exploited. He is correct, however, in his understanding that the managers' blurring of the lines between business and personal relationships is a particularly difficult barrier to advancement for non-traditional workers.

🐘 *Ability to select an appropriate response.* Mark's stereotyping of whites and his assumption that racism is a significant factor in his current situation is hindering his diversity management effectiveness. His assumption of ill will or ignorance on the part of all whites unnecessarily excludes them as possible sources of support, thus reducing the odds that he will compete successfully for promotion.

This leaves him with little choice but to isolate (by refusing to take his managers' relationship suggestions), tolerate (interact superficially), or exclude (threaten to leave) whites. Isolation hasn't worked. Toleration is seen as insufficient in his organization. Threatening to leave is unlikely to garner support. All of these options may work against his best interests and leave him feeling defeated.

WHAT'S NEXT FOR MARK?

Mark has several options. He can leave the company, and he may well do so. But his belief that expectations will be similar throughout corporate America means he won't leave in hopes of avoiding relationship requirements. He will leave instead in search of greater opportunity.

Key to progressing as he wishes in the next organization would be his willingness to rethink some core inclusion and race-related issues and to gain a better understanding of the nature and scope of genuine diversity.

He can tolerate the "requirements" mixture. In this instance, Mark would acknowledge the two tiers of requirements but make relatively little effort to satisfy those related to relationships and accept the consequences. He probably would continue to do well as a sales representative and receive substantial compensation, but he would forgo his dream of entering into the managerial ranks.

He could stay and assimilate around the relationships requirement. He would have to be willing to build relationships with those managers with whom he has been unhappy, as well as with peers. This would require letting go of resentments toward the managers who didn't support his promotion. Assuming responsibility for his role in the promotion disappointment would be a start in this direction.

Mark has considerable talent and ambition. His ability to parlay these into personal and organizational advantages will rest considerably on his willingness to address his personal approach to diversity in ways that help him to become more diversity mature.

🐘 8 🐘

The Pioneering Elephants: Joan and Richard

Joan's Story

I am a white woman in my late forties. I came to this company nearly twenty years ago because I wanted experience with a large company. Before that I had worked for only small to medium-sized companies. My experiences in these companies left something to be desired.

The first company I worked for was very paternalistically managed. It had an old ''company store'' mentality: ''We'll take care of you. We'll be your security.'' It was a very comfortable environment to work in, but it wasn't diverse at all. With one exception, the management was all white males. It felt like a caste system. I'm sure there was a color caste, but it didn't affect me. The caste system I noticed was mostly gender related. It was a work environment where employees weren't given equal consideration for career opportunities.

I left there to work in a start-up entrepreneurial environment where everything was focused on expanding the business. It was very disheartening to see how employees were mistreated for the sake of growing the business. Employees were regarded as expendable commodities.

Current Company

I was looking for a more employee-friendly company. I also felt that I needed to move to a much larger company—one that would allow room for development and movement—if I wanted to grow professionally. A company the size of this one provided that kind of mobility.

This is a fast-paced, highly flexible, relatively nonhierarchical organization. The culture values perfection—doing the right things right. There's a great deal of emphasis on risk taking but very little tolerance for error. There are career consequences if you fall short of the mark.

There is also a strong work ethic in this company. Employees are very loyal and willing to work long hours. That's across the board.

Demographic diversity is important. We're a large consumer products company. We can't meet the needs of our customers unless we have employees who understand the diversity of those customers.

In some ways the company is doing a very good job of creating the necessary demographics. Walk the halls of the building, and you see diversity among our employees. In other respects, we still have room for improvement. Minorities and women are relatively well represented at different levels in certain departments, but we fall short in others. Women appear to be represented more adequately than minorities. We have female officers and department heads but not so many minorities in these positions.

Our shortcoming in representation in key positions is historical—our practice has been to promote from within. But now it's also because the organization is becoming flatter. Opportunities for upper mobility are few.

Still, the company has enjoyed a reputation for being a very desirable place to work. We haven't had any difficulty attracting diverse and talented people. However, as we try to recruit the future workforce, we find that today's job candidates want instant financial reward. Having a future equity position in the company doesn't have the same appeal for them as it does for those of us who've been here awhile.

Fitting In to the Organization

Most of my initial expectations have been met and exceeded. Certainly I've had the mobility I sought. I have progressed very nicely during my years in human resources (HR) with the company, moving from compensation to a generalist role and eventually being promoted to a division vice president job.

Several years into that job, the position was eliminated. Since then I have taken on two project assignments; one heading up a cross-functional new products development team and the other a customer relations project. These last two moves have been nontraditional in the sense of career progression. They've also been lateral in terms of job level.

The elimination of the vice president of HR job had personal as well as career implications. I kept my officer status and the privileges that come with that, but I no longer have positional power. I've had to redefine what and who I am, and to answer the question, "How will I be viewed now that I no longer have that positional power?" I can now accept the fact that what happened to me is not unique. It's part of a trend; companies are evolving, and as they do, they de-layer and consolidate. I know not to take it personally.

The experience has affected how I will manage my career from here on. I have become much more adept at asking questions and probing for answers as opposed to leaving my career entirely in the hands of others. It has also caused me to look back over my career to see what and how I might have done things differently.

I believe that I should have sought the help of others more often than I did. In this company, mentors, who serve as both guides and advocates, are important to success. The people who are seen as movers and shakers have had the good fortune of coming in under one of the key senior managers and benefiting from their guidance.

The mentoring system here is informal and the relationships unstructured. Mentoring usually comes in the form of advice from a peer or a manager who says, "Be careful how you approach this or that"—an advise-and-counsel kind of role. Finding an effective mentor can be difficult. Coming in from the outside, it's hard to know who the key influencers are. You have to be careful not to connect up with people who are not politically savvy lest you find yourself guilty by association. I've never really had a long-term mentor, although I've had good managers who taught and coached me well.

I also think that both the company's expectations of women and my response to these expectations may have created obstacles for me. This is not a confrontational culture. As a woman in this culture, you learn not to be too direct. Yet my male counterparts are comfortable being assertive, even aggressive. They don't worry about whether they're going to step on somebody's toes or how their behavior might be interpreted. They simply act and ask forgiveness later.

I'm not sure how much the culture influenced my behavior to be somewhat guarded and tentative, or whether it was due to my own concern about how I was coming across to people.

Women coming into the company today aren't as likely to have that dilemma. Those in their late twenties and early thirties are far more aggressive. They speak out if there is something that they do not like or they're impatient with. They call it as they see it, and they make no apologies for it. These women run up against senior managers who aren't comfortable with that type of behavior but don't quite know what to do about it. Furthermore, it's not just younger women, white and black, who are more aggressive. Younger men are the same. If they're in that age group, they just go for it; they're not shy about speaking their minds.

This aggressiveness causes discomfort among the majority here—those in their forties and fifties. It's the age-old attitude of "been there, done that." They see these younger employees come along and think they're going to change things overnight and know that it isn't going to happen that quickly. When these younger employees are not able to make any headway, they eventually assimilate and go along with the rest.

The Workplace as a Source of Diversity Learning

In the past four years, the need to operate without positional power has provided some new learning about diversity for me.

I define diversity as a multiplicity of thoughts and opinions and viewpoints. I'm much less likely to put a color, gender, race, age, or disability face on it.

My most powerful experience with diversity as multiplicity came when I headed up the new products project. I found myself out of the HR comfort zone and into the totally foreign world of new products development, faced with a very aggressive time line. I had to rely on people who knew more about the subject matter than I did—people who had expertise with customers, information technology, product development, competitors, and market trends.

The makeup of the team was diverse. There were whites and blacks. Some were in their sixties, others in their twenties. Even more important was the way they viewed the project. Marketing, sales, research, information systems, human resources, and finance people all have a way of approaching their respective disciplines. They bring different perspectives and convictions as a result of what it takes to be successful in their fields. They were all very good at what they did. But getting them to work together toward a common objective was very difficult. My HR facilitation skills came in handy.

There definitely was conflict—members of the various teams wanting to hold on to their functional thinking and approaches. For a while it seemed unlikely that any common ground could be reached. Each kept going in a different direction and trying to convince the others to join them.

In order to resolve these conflicts and stay on the timetable, I had to sort out the best way to keep the project moving without disenfranchising anyone. It was stressful and difficult. I had to rely on people influencing other people to change their minds, compromise, or buy into a consensus. It wouldn't have been possible without getting a commitment about where we wanted to end up. Once everyone agreed to that, it was easier to find cohesion. Even then, it didn't come together naturally. We had to work at it.

The situation was exasperating, frustrating, and threatening. But ultimately, it was an invigorating, successful, and exciting experience. I learned a lot about diversity, although at the time it felt like conflict, not diversity. I also became a much stronger, better person and a better leader as a result of it.

I'm not sure I could have had this kind of experience working within an HR environment. For this situation I needed an interdisciplinary context. Had I been working within an HR environment, I would have been with people who came from disciplines that I was comfortable and familiar with. The diverseness of process and results would have been less likely to occur.

In addition, I probably wouldn't have been as open to diversity in a more familiar context. My comfort with the subject matter would have made me more likely to rely on the way I always handled things, because it would have been second nature to me.

In that interdisciplinary situation, I knew where we had to end up, but I had only a vague idea of how we were going to get there. I was totally out of my element. That forced me to figure out how to navigate through all of the diversity of opinions, skills, and experiences.

Current Diversity Situation

Currently I am testing my diversity skills in a project around a training initiative. As was true in the earlier situation, I've been given responsibility but not direct authority. The team sees me as a peer. My role is to coordinate and work behind the scenes.

I'm labeling the project a diversity situation because the success of the project depends on three people. One is a young white male who is relatively new to the company. He's very bright, but he doesn't want to take the time to listen and understand the needs of others on the team. The second person has been with the company a long time and is feeling unappreciated and undervalued. Yet his experience is critical to the project. The third person is a young white female. She is bright, temperamental, and wants to make certain that her specific contribution to the project is duly recognized.

Getting these people to come together and work in a collaborative fashion is a real challenge. None of them appears to think beyond what's in it for them. They talk the "team" stuff, but it is very easy to get off track when their individual agendas come to the forefront.

In both this and the earlier situation, I've relied on one constant. That's my inherent tendency to seek out resolution and compromise. It's important to me to gain consensus and somehow maintain camaraderie.

When I've been able to do that, I've been effective. The times when I've not been effective have been when I had a very limited time to accomplish something, and I didn't have the luxury of getting everyone's buy-in. I had to make a decision. It's to be expected that people will feel disenfranchised—ignored and slighted.

JOAN AS SKILLED DIVERSITY RESPONDENT

Joan stands at a crossroads in her career. In the past, she experienced success and significant upward mobility with her company. Now, however, she has been sidelined. She performs meaningful support work, and she retains her vice presidential title and the trappings of success. However, she lacks organizational power and she is no longer is in contention for promotions and greater responsibility.

Joan's Diversity Maturity

Accepts Responsibility

Joan is more reflective about diversity than she was in the past. She reflects and speculates on her responses to diversity mixtures. In doing so, she replays, analyzes, learns, and modifies her approach in a way that she may not have done at an earlier point in her career, a clear indication of a process of maturing. In addition, she consciously uses diversity principles to address diversity within her work groups. She has not, however, attempted to expand her personal concern and skills into greater organizational diversity effectiveness.

Demonstrates Contextual Knowledge

The Business Motive. Joan demonstrates understanding of the business motive both when she speaks generally about the need to understand and reflect the company's diverse customers and more specifically about her projects during the past four years. She notes that agreement on the final outcome (business requirements) was essential to enabling her very diverse and divisive group to work successfully together. She also notes her lack of success when she has failed to elicit the opinions of all project participants. Joan not only experiences the compelling business motive for addressing diversity when working without organizational power. She sees this ability as key to her continued success in her career.

Conceptual Clarity About Diversity. Joan has made considerable progress in differentiating inclusion from diversity in the past four years. She has moved beyond believing that demographic characteristics are the only significant aspects of diversity to seeing diversity as a multiplicity that includes thoughts, viewpoints, and behaviors. And she has learned that functional diversity, with its many implications, can have a powerful impact. Further, she has experienced how moving out of one's comfort zone encourages facility with diversity management. Hers is not merely theoretical knowledge. She has learned it in the trenches.

Is Comfortable With Diversity Tension

In the past, Joan appears to have avoided acknowledging or addressing diversity tension when able to do this. During the past four years, however, she has lived in its midst. She is justifiably proud of her ability to work with very diverse people, address the tensions that accompany this diversity, and provide the informal leadership that allows them to accomplish their goals in the midst of the inevitable misunderstandings and disagreements.

Core Diversity Skills

🐘 *Ability to recognize diversity mixtures.* Joan recognizes a number of diversity mixtures: organizational status, gender, age, and functions. She reports reflecting intensely on organizational status and gender and has acted in awareness of age and functional diversity.

🐘 *Ability to analyze the mixtures and related tensions.* Joan does not systematically analyze diversity mixtures and their tensions to determine which have the most potential impact on the company's ability to meet its objectives. Her response remains more personal and focused within her specific work group.

🐘 *Ability to choose a course of action.* Joan has responded to several identified mixtures. Among these are the following.

▪ *Past and current status.* For Joan, a key mixture is her past and current status and resulting self-perception. In the past, she possessed positional power and saw herself as managing and controlling. Now she lacks positional power. She views herself as learning, teaching, and facilitating. In the past, she headed departments. Now she works on a project-by-project basis, facilitating the work of cross-functional groups and mentoring younger people. She believes she has learned much about the company, and she stands ready to share her knowledge and understanding.

Joan accepts and understands the similarities and differences between her past and present status. Common to both, for example, is her desire to foster the continued well-being of the company in the interest of her potential to generate personal wealth.

To this end, Joan has chosen a "foster mutual adaptation" stance with respect to her two statuses. She is crafting a role that reflects the realities and meets the requirements of both. The result has been considerable personal growth. She has deepened her understanding of the big picture and corporate dynamics, and she has a greater appreciation for diversity and diversity management.

Her personal growth and current success have not been easily won. She still experiences the tension related to the two statuses and feels a sense of loss.

Ironically, her fall from power has given her perspectives and skills that would serve her well as a formal leader and manager. But senior executives and leaders aren't likely to let her back in the field, so she has developed a way of contributing in the context of new realities. She has managed the diversity of her past and current status well.

• *Gender.* Joan has always recognized the gender issue, but she suppressed her awareness of this mixture while moving up the organizational ladder. Once this movement was stopped, she included the gender mixture in her search for answers as to what had gone wrong.

Was her earlier suppression appropriate? In one respect it was. It eliminated what could have been a distraction. She no doubt believed, "As long as I do my job, it really shouldn't matter." And it didn't for a significant period of time. But in another respect it wasn't. It put her out of touch with the reality of gender issues, mentoring, and the dynamics of power. By her own account, she may have survived had she understood these issues better.

Yet it is not her suppression that is the critical issue. It was her failure to surface the issue every so often and look at its implications. A combination of suppression and periodic reassessment of the gender issue would have served Joan better.

• *Age.* Most people suppress the reality of aging and its accompanying dynamics, and are blindsided when they experience it. Joan may be an exception. She seems to grasp the realities and requirements well enough to accept change with grace. By fostering mutual adaptation, she should manage this mixture well.

• *Functional diversity.* For much of her career, Joan managed within an HR perspective. Currently she works on cross-functional teams. In the past, HR expertise was the basis for her authority. Now the value of this expertise is dependent on the project. Of more importance is her ability to address and reconcile a multiplicity of thoughts, opinions, and perspectives.

In doing this, she says, she has "relied on one constant: my inherent tendency to seek out resolution and compromise." The success of this approach may depend on how she approaches her goal of resolution. If she chooses an understanding differences approach, as she has in the past, the strategy is likely to be inadequate, as issues of informal power, accommodation, and privilege exert a covert influence. The choice of a foster mutual adaptation approach should be more successful as organizational requirements take center stage. Joan may have to struggle as she balances a mixture of what may have worked in her past circumstances with what is more viable now.

WHAT'S NEXT FOR JOAN?

In general, Joan has responded well—though not perfectly—to diversity mixtures. She displays several attributes that suggest that her capability to address diversity well will continue to grow.

In the immediate future, Joan will likely continue to serve as a facilitator in numerous cross-functional settings. These opportunities for learning should greatly strengthen the diversity management skills that she needs as she moves to place the finishing touches on a successful career.

Richard's Story

I am an African American man. I've worked in high-tech industries for twenty-two years and have been with this company the past fifteen years. I've always had a passion for the HR field. It goes back to the summer of my junior year when I returned to my parents' home and worked on the assembly line of a manufacturing plant.

Working conditions were pretty bad. We worked fifty-five minutes an hour with a five-minute break and had a fifteen-minute break for lunch. I saw that the workers were very smart and could figure out how to break down a line whenever they got tired and needed to rest. Then the engineers would come over and scratch their heads, trying to figure out what went wrong. Of course, they never asked us, because we weren't educated or smart.

At first I was amused. Then I realized the workers were essentially putting themselves out of a job by raising the cost of their products, and the managers were not utilizing the people who were closest to the process and knew the most. That's when I discovered the power of human resources. Companies that could get the two groups to work together in the same direction would be the companies that would succeed.

I came to Raleigh/Durham as a site manager in a complex that holds about 2,000 employees. When I describe my job, I say, "I'm responsible for the atmosphere here. If you don't have atmosphere, you die. If you have it, you don't notice it." When I got here, an HR and an operations manager reported to me. When the HR manager retired, I didn't replace him. I just started wearing both hats. Holding on to the HR job gave me a body of expertise where I am the direct authority. It gave me my own turf.

When I wear my site manager's hat, I'm more like a landlord for a bunch of different tenants who don't always get along. If there's an issue between internal organizations, I am the arbiter. I manage the community-company atmosphere by making decisions as to how the company will be presented as well.

The Organization

Most of what attracted me to this company has turned out to be true. Unfortunately the only area where it isn't progressive is diversity. This failing goes against some of my deepest beliefs. To me, diversity is being proud of all the things that make us who we are: economic background, educational background, race and gender, rural versus city, and so on. I believe that all of us have the ability to make unique contributions because of our backgrounds and characteristics. So I believe in honoring everything that we bring to the table. That's what makes us us. I also believe in judging people by their actions and results.

Importance of Assimilation

This is an organization where you can be successful if you can assimilate. If you have the same interests and do the same things, there is no problem. But if you try to hold on to what, in the end, makes you unique, that can become an issue. For example, there's an assumption that everyone lives in the suburbs, is heterosexual, and wants 2.2 kids and a dog. In addition, people here tend to vote Republican, conservative. Not everybody fits into the paradigm. Even in a roomful of white males, it doesn't take long to realize that there are differences. There are the ones who didn't go to a prestige school, the ones whose father wasn't an engineer. There are all kinds of differences. But those types of differences are a little easier for people to submerge and act ``as if.'' And that's important. If you give the appearance of fitting the mold, that's acceptable. I have found that to the extent that I fit in, it's no problem.

Of course, I usually don't. I've always lived in urban areas; I don't vote Republican; I'm a person of color and a gay man. The organization's discomfort with diversity has been a personal cross to bear. It has been frustrating. But I have to remind myself that I've been here nineteen years, and I don't really know what it's like on the outside. Maybe this is as good as it gets. Also, there has been progress, some of which has benefited me. When I came to North Carolina, I came out as a gay male. I've had no problems with that, at least not to my face. My management has been very supportive. I know that at one time that would not have been the case.

Diversity Struggles

Yet the company still struggles with racial diversity. That has been personally challenging. The bad part is that sometimes I feel I'm the only one carrying the banner. When I bring the topic of diversity up, I feel, though I don't see, people's eyes rolling ``Here he goes again.'' That's an ongoing issue.

I'm particularly frustrated when people attempt to imply that what happens to African Americans doesn't really apply to me. I react negatively when people say, ``When I look at you, I don't see color.'' Well, what does that mean? Am I white? I can't imagine them saying that with gender. I can't imagine them saying, ``I don't even see a man when I see you. I just see a human being.'' To me, that just shows the denial. It's a roundabout way of saying they see me as them. So I think, ``I must not be acting black enough.''

There is denial of what the environment is like for people of color and others who don't fit the mold as well. Those who are different suffer. White employees who don't fit the mold see it clearly too. It's a matter of fitting the image, not just a race thing.

Still, even the language used to discuss minorities and women suggests a negative perception. We always talk about developing minorities and women. This perpetuates the notion that the only developing needed is with people who aren't white males. Managers in this company must take a diversity class, although there's no requirement that the rank and file do so. To me, that would be a milestone. It would show our maturation in this journey to say that every employee needs this sort of training to get past the notion that there's nothing wrong with *them*; it's those *others* who need fixing.

This need is particularly evident in the results of our employee surveys. There's always a section that asks people to write about whatever they want. Because it's an anonymous process, a lot of sexist, racist, homophobic comments come out. The quantity and strength of these comments have really surprised me and let me know that racism, sexism, and the other isms have gone underground rather than gone away. We really are a microcosm of the larger community. There are a lot of people walking around who are smiling on the outside but below that are feeling that all of the openings are going to people of color, and we're shoving a gay and lesbian agenda down their throat. We've got to give these people an avenue to discuss their concerns because that's the only way they are going to grow.

Deceiving Appearances

It's very hard to convince people that the culture needs to change. They look at me and say, ``You're here; you've been successful. You're proof that we are diverse.'' Of course, *I* don't see it that way. It doesn't take a genius in organizational behavior to know that the power is in the revenue-generating part of the organization. Administration, with its human resources, finance, and other departments, is an overhead. You'll find more diversity in those functions than you will in the R&D, manufacturing, and line functions. That's not unique to this organization. Historically, diversity does start in the administrative functions. Then folks in these functions boost the others over the wall. We just haven't gotten to that stage in this organization.

My frustration and challenge have been to see more diversity in the technical areas or in the places where the real power lies. One way I do that is to insist on defining my position as it is. My business card says "general manager." But I don't like to use that title. I think it's an anomaly. In this organization, general managers have profit and loss responsibility. Typically they have product strategy responsibilities as well. I don't have these responsibilities. So I use "site manager" instead. I don't want the organization to say, "We have an African American general manager," implying that I have the power to make big money and product decisions. I'm sure that happens, but I don't validate it.

I also try to create a culture that encourages diversity in technical or power areas by using myself as a model. My hope is that my willingness to come out and acknowledge differences I don't have to acknowledge, such as my sexual orientation, will give others permission to accept and be proud and admit that they're different too—whatever that difference might be.

When I was in the Boston area, I lost about eight friends to AIDS over a two-year period. That put things in perspective. It made me realize that the journey here is too brief to be living by other people's standards. When they close the lid on me, I don't want a lot of regrets out there.

The Link Between Personal Experiences and Career Success

Interestingly, some of my negative experiences as a different person have helped me to be successful in my work. They have taught me, for example, to relate to people at whatever level they are on without their feeling threatened. People who know I disagree with them still feel safe expressing their views. And it's not something I have to force because their views are valid for them.

Recently a group of employees came to me and said, "We can have gay and lesbian groups; we can have this and that. Why can't we have Bible study groups?" I said, "You can, so long as you focus on individual development. I don't want you to come back saying the company should or shouldn't do this or that." The people who wanted the group were stunned. They probably thought that I, as a gay man, would never allow it to happen.

Others were stunned as well. All sorts of people said, "No, no, we don't do religious groups." I just kept replying, "All we're saying is that these people can use the conference room on their own time."

The gay and lesbian group was particularly upset because they associated the Bible study with the Moral Majority and that kind of thing. But I told them, "You're stereotyping too. Just because somebody wants Bible study doesn't necessarily make him or her homophobic."

I think that you gain a different insight when you have experienced negative treatment for something over which you have no choice—something that is just a function of who you are. In truth, I experience a double whammy. As an African American, I have to deal with the homophobia within the black community, and there's still racism within the gay and lesbian community. I constantly see examples of how people can be mistreated for something that is no choice of their own.

Honoring the Past by Making a Contribution

My unhappiness about the company's failings around diversity doesn't mean I'm not committed to making a contribution here. I am. In fact, this commitment was strengthened over the past six years. It began when my father, who was dying, talked more about his life as a young black man than he ever had before. He told me that he had earned an electrician's degree in the 1950s and applied to Ohio Bell, only to see the guy throw his application in the wastebasket as he went out the door. So he worked at a steel mill for thirty years and retired as a foreman. My father was just as intelligent as I am and could have been just as successful in a corporate environment if he had had the opportunity.

He didn't live to see me enjoy my success in North Carolina, but my uncle did. He remembers living in this area as a child. He tells me of their early days and marvels at the things I do. "Appalachia Park? We couldn't go to Appalachia Park," he says. When I told him I sat in the president's box at a Duke game, he said, "We used to stay off the streets after a Duke game because somebody would get drunk and rough us up." These were things I didn't know. My parents didn't teach racial hate. In fact, we were so insulated against racism that it wasn't until the riots in the 1960s, when I was fourteen or fifteen, that I even thought, "Why is everybody so upset?"

Knowing the experiences of my family members has given me a real sense that I owe it to my father and grandparents to build on the foundation that they laid for me. It has encouraged me to learn more about my earlier ancestors as well. I've been to Senegal. When I went through the area where the slaves and the ship owners set sail, it gave me a sense that I owe it to my ancestors to make a difference. Many of them just gave up and jumped overboard. The ones who produced me are the ones who had the strongest will to live.

All of these things put a perspective on the racism that I experience. At least I'm not dealing with life-and-death issues or being kept from walking down the street. Understanding my past helps me to understand how fortunate I am. It also gives me the courage and motivation to deal with these issues, so hopefully the next generation, my nephews, won't have to contend with what I'm dealing with.

One way I encourage change is to strive to make this organization a more inclusive place to work. I want to create the kind of environment where diversity—defined as differences in ways of thinking as well as race and gender and the other characteristics we generally think of—thrives.

I want an environment that allows somebody who is part of a work group to express his or her ideas no matter how far in left field the person may seem to be, in an environment where people don't submerge themselves because they think it's the only way to succeed.

Managing the Rage

Knowing that things are better for me than for my ancestors doesn't keep me from feeling rage at some of the things I do experience. But I've found there's no place to express this rage. For example, I'd like to be able to go to a family gathering and complain about the issues I'm dealing with within the organization. But my cousins and siblings, most of whom didn't graduate from college, would not understand. They see my W-2 and ask, "What's your problem?" If I went to whites, they'd say, "What's your problem? You're at a higher level than we are." So it's hard to know how to respond. What do you do with the rage you don't have permission to express?

Advice to Different People

One way I try to help people defined as different is to offer some suggestions for enhancing their organizational success. I say, "You must first understand the rules of the game and balance whether the rewards are worth the price you will have to pay. Because there is a price. When you work in any organization, some degree of conformity is required. You have to decide. It's your right to choose to be inflexible. But it's not logical to think you can do so and still get the rewards of the organization." If you do choose to be flexible, you must decide how far you're willing to go. You may decide the corporate world is not for you and you'd rather work for yourself. But that's much harder and entails a lot more risk.

I also tell them, "When negative things happen to you, let your difference be the last thing you come to in assigning the cause." I tell black employees in particular, "You know, somebody can dislike you and like the rest of us. So, don't automatically jump to that." The other thing I say is, "You've got to be prepared." Years of being involved in hiring and staffing decisions have convinced me that people are much more willing to take a chance on somebody who looks or acts like them. When you don't fit the norm, you've got to have the validations up front, and it has to be exactly what they are looking for.

The Necessity to Self-Assess

I know that creating an environment that values and honors diversity will continue to be a tough task. I'm not always sure I'm up to it. My concern that people are just giving lip-service to diversity or that I'm not being forceful or revolutionary enough keeps me up at night. Should I have left and gone to a smaller company or gone into the diversity field itself—gone into something that would more directly affect the things that are important? Have I sold out? It's something I have to assess periodically.

RICHARD AS EFFECTIVE DIVERSITY RESPONDENT

Richard is one of the highest-ranking blacks in his company and a man who enjoys his job. He conveys commitment to his work and a sense of contentment with who he is. He is, by all accounts, a successful individual. He is also a man who worries about the value of his accomplishments and his ability to make a difference. And he continues to struggle with his rage and the lack of appropriate places and ways to express it.

Richard is an elephant who is successful in a giraffe's house. At issue is the personal cost to him. At this career crossroads, Richard has redefined his priorities and is determining how to achieve his mixture of work/life objectives. He thinks that his current position may be as good as it gets, but he sometimes wonders if he could realize more of his agenda elsewhere.

Richard's Diversity Maturity

Accepts Responsibility

Clearly Richard has thought long and hard about differences and their possible consequences. He accepts personal responsibility for addressing diversity effectively and is remarkably successful at doing so. He accepts responsibility for improving his organization's diversity effectiveness as well. He works to help his company understand the pain its culture creates for those who are qualified and different. He seeks to help individuals acknowledge and express their differences, and uses himself as a model. Indeed, achieving personal and organizational diversity effectiveness are two aspects of Richard's larger mission: ensuring that those who follow him don't experience the negative effects of the isms.

Demonstrates Contextual Knowledge

An Understanding of Self. Richard knows who he is and what he hopes to accomplish. He continues to question and challenge himself and to assess his life on an ongoing basis. He is also willing to disclose who he is, even when doing so makes his life more complex.

The Business Motive. Richard's desire to minimize the pain and suffering of those who are different has left him little time to identify and articulate the business and viability benefits of diversity for the organization. Once he understands and communicates the business motive, he can move to a more sophisticated posture on differences. His concern with attaining acceptance of all differences has inhibited him from differentiating among differences. This leaves the impression that all differences are okay. But from an organizational perspective, this is decidedly not so. Within a given set of business objectives and requirements, all differences are not acceptable. Differences that contribute to the ability to meet requirements are unconditionally accepted. Those with no direct impact on this ability are conditionally accepted. Those that prevent the organization from meeting its objectives are unacceptable. Without these distinctions, conversations around differences and diversity can become unnecessarily vague.

Once clear about the nature of diversity and inclusion and better able to articulate the business motive, Richard can use his workplace experiences as personal learning labs. His responsibilities require that he deal with line and staff, multiple organizational units, and company-community diversity mixtures, and he appears to do so very well. Yet he seems not to see these mixtures as diversity issues, a shortsightedness that keeps him from benefiting from his skills in these areas. By reflecting on and analyzing his responses to these mixtures, he can transfer his learning from these low-tension mixtures to the more volatile race and sexual orientation mixtures. He can urge his managers to do the same. If he can get the organization into a learning mode around these business mixtures, progress with the others might go more rapidly. The more he can make diversity the organization's issue as well as his own, the greater the likelihood that he can help his company become more diversity-effective.

Conceptual Clarity About Diversity. Richard continues his ongoing growth as an effective diversity respondent. He demonstrates this growth in his strong grasp of differences and their consequences in the workplace, and in his expansion of differences beyond traditional workforce dimensions. He demonstrates it in his understanding that differences exist within and also across racial groups. This growth is clear in his understanding of what the focus on assimilation costs his company as well.

However, Richard would benefit from greater conceptual clarity. He often talks as if diversity and inclusiveness are interchangeable. They are not. He is most concerned about inclusiveness. He focuses on inclusion, for example, when he is concerned that people with different demographic characteristics are included in the workplace. Yet he clearly desires diversity—the expression of cognitive and behavioral differences—as well. Both are worthy goals, and they are often (though not always) interrelated. What's important to his ability to achieve his larger mission is to distinguish clearly between the two.

Richard also experiences confusion about differences and diversity. He uses the words as if they were the same. People can demonstrate very different demographic characteristics and behave in very similar ways (offer little behavior diversity).

Core Diversity Skills

🖪 *Ability to identify diversity mixtures.* Richard's world is multifaceted and multidimensional, filled with a plethora of diversity mixtures: sexual orientation, race, marital status, socio-economic background, gender, union and non-union, work/life, political views, urban and suburban, religion, historical aware-ness, organizational units, staff and line, and community and company. All of these mixtures currently influence him, but three have a special claim on his attention: sexual orientation, race, and work/life mixtures.

Richard speaks poignantly of the tensions he lives with every day, tensions that derive from two of his significant mixtures: the "double whammy" of homophobia in the black community and racism in the gay community. His personal ex-periences with discrimination and his desire that others be spared this pain motivate him to give these mixtures top billing.

◀ *Ability to analyze the mixtures and related tensions.* Within the organization, there is a cost for doing so. His focus on these mixtures prevents him from asking the question, "What diver-sity mixture and tension is likely to prevent me from meeting business requirements in this specific situation?" Given his re-sponsibilities, it is likely that the organizational unit-commu-nity-company mixtures and tensions are often key. In fact, Richard reports that he manages friction among these entities every day.

Yet his focus on the isms prevents him from seeing these as significant diversity mixtures. This, in turn, keeps him from transferring his impressive skills in getting different entities to work together for the benefit of the organization to the demo-graphic mixture arena that so engages him. It prevents him from communicating this analogy to others in the organization as well. The result is a split in his mind and those of his cohorts. On the one hand, he manages *workplace* diversity in ways that allow him to achieve business requirements. On the other hand, he manages *workforce* diversity in ways that leave others unaware of the organizational benefits of including people of different demographic characteristics and allowing them to express their differences. This inadvertently works against achieving his di-versity goals.

◀ *Ability to select an appropriate response.* Richard's response to sexual orientation and racial diversity has evolved. Historically he relied on assimilation and suppression—two responses that share a willingness to play "let's pretend there aren't differences or that these differences don't count."

For years he assimilated to company norms and concealed his sexual orientation while at work, although he was more open when away from the workplace. Such a split must have had a considerable cost. Assimilation and suppression, however, have their advantages, and they can be hard to give up. It took some wrenching personal experiences for Richard to abandon these diversity choices. As he became aware of his father's pain and anger and his racial ancestors' misery, his perspective changed. He became committed to making a difference by building on their efforts. His arena for this is the organization. His goals are a more inclusive workplace and society. To accomplish this requires more boldness around racial diversity than was characteristic of his earlier choices. Indeed, Richard struggles to abandon suppression around racial diversity, but the more he struggles to surface his rage, the more his significant others resist. He may inadvertently arrive at segregation and isolation or toleration on this diversity dimension. If so, he will almost certainly experience even higher levels of frustration. To avoid this scenario, he must adapt creative ways to convey racial challenges that concern him.

The loss of his friends to AIDS also led Richard to make new choices about sexual orientation diversity. He abandoned suppression, determined to live by his own, not others', rules. Currently he practices fostering mutual adaptation with respect to sexual orientation and work/life diversity. He works to gain greater acceptance and inclusiveness for gays and lesbians and greater appreciation for their contributions.

Richard carries on discussions on work/life diversity with himself. He wonders how he can honor his father and ancestors and whether he can do this effectively in a corporate environment. He strives to identify his life requirements and to see if his current choices will allow him to meet them. His goal is to achieve a mutual adaptation resolution with respect to work/life. He is early in the process, but he is determined to address the complexity brought about by his new perspectives.

WHAT'S NEXT FOR RICHARD?

Richard's history of and propensity toward personal growth make it hard to predict exactly where he will go from here. Some things, however, do seem likely. He will continue to work toward greater personal clarity and self-expression and to care deeply about inclusion and diversity issues. He will continue to conduct a cost-benefit analysis on the price of career success as well.

His ability to get his company to take diversity as seriously as he does will depend in large part on his ability to position diversity management as essential to organizational success.

9

Diversity Effectiveness: The Challenges for Elephants

The elephant experience may be totally negative. It may be tolerable. It may even be positive. To be an elephant in a giraffe's house is not necessarily an unrewarding experience, but it is likely always to be characterized by the tension that comes with being an outsider, from occupying another's house. For elephants, the critical question becomes, "Can I meet my needs here, or would I be better off in someone else's house?"

The answer may depend as much on the elephant as on the giraffes. Those who believe they must avoid all elephant experiences are in for some rude surprises. Those who believe they cannot accomplish meaningful goals because of their elephant status can expect to achieve little.

A better approach is to assume, unless proven otherwise, that it is possible to respond to giraffe-elephant situations in ways that maximize productivity and minimize the potential negative impact of the elephant experience. This may not always work, and it may still be necessary to go elsewhere to achieve your maximum potential. But starting with optimistic assumptions and acting on them will increase the likelihood of turning the elephant experience into a personal and organizational triumph.

CHALLENGES TO ELEPHANTS

Elephants who hope to become effective diversity respondents must address several critical tasks and meet several personal and organizational challenges.

Identifying Personal Requirements

Perhaps the biggest challenge for elephants is being clear about requirements. The task is to meet their own while accommodating the head giraffe's and the organization's requirements. This is vital. As long as the elephant, the organization, and the head giraffe get their requirements met, they are likely to remain together. Should one or more decide that these requirements won't be met, one party will have to leave, and that is usually the elephant.

To identify requirements, elephants must begin with themselves. They must ask, "What are my bottom-line requirements?" That means separating out the "nice-to-haves": the personal preferences, the conveniences, the habits. To illustrate the difference, let us draw a hypothetical example.

Suppose you are ready to make a career change. You have satisfied the necessary educational requirements for a highly technical job. Now you want an opportunity to hone your skills, and you have concluded the best way to do that is to work under a skilled and respected technician.

You enjoy working at your current location. The people are friendly and the culture informal. You also like the fact that you can walk to work. You apply for a posted position in your new field and are offered the job. In one respect, it's perfect. It will allow you to work under a recognized pro. But there are costs. The position is located across town, and you're told that the master technician is known to be testy.

If you have accurately identified your requirements, you need to accept the job. Pleasant people are a preference, a close-by workplace a convenience. The only real requirement is the opportunity to work under a pro.

While the decisions may change, the principle remains constant. Few jobs—or anything else, for that matter—meet all of our wishes. The critical task is to identify requirements—those things that are essential.

This is never easy for anyone, but it's harder for elephants in a giraffe's house to do so than for their giraffe peers. For one thing, they may have to subsume some of their personal requirements simply to get the job. Once there, they are often expected to surrender other requirements in the name of fitting in. Most companies and head giraffes reward assimilation and have little desire to focus on differences.

Assimilation can be difficult for elephants. Some respond by denying to themselves and others that significant differences exist. Denial is in play, for example, when racial or ethnic elephants insist that affirmative action has not benefited them. To admit to such benefits would highlight the elephant status they are seeking to shed.

Two of the interviewed elephants are evidence of this. Ray (Chapter 6) downplays racial and ethnic differences as part of his strategy for achieving his career goals. At this point, he sees his strategy as working. Mark (Chapter 7) joined his company with great expectations and with no exploration of diversity issues he might encounter. At first, this decision made sense. Mark performed well, and the company rewarded him financially. It was only when he sought promotions that differences around social requirements emerged, to Mark's great dismay.

Another challenge for elephants in identifying their personal requirements is the need to examine themselves. Many people, elephants or not, lack practice and skill with introspection. Young elephants may be particularly loath to spend time looking within themselves. They think that they have so much to do and so little time to do it, and so they depend on others to tell them what they require. They may acknowledge their error only when events make it clear that their genuine requirements haven't been met. Richard (Chapter 8) provides an example. It took the traumatic loss of friends and a profound awakening to his historical roots before he defined his own requirements. Carol, too, became more focused on her own requirements after being disappointed.

Elephants must continuously ask, "Who am I? Who am I becoming? Who do I want to become?" Those who don't ask these questions frequently realize with a shock that they don't recognize or like the person they have become.

Identifying Other People's and Organizations' Requirements

As if identifying their personal requirements and expectations were not challenge enough, elephants must also identify those of their organizations and head giraffe. The experiences of Mark, Debra (Chapter 7), and Joan (Chapter 8) suggest that this can be difficult.

Mark and Debra discovered social requirements after joining their companies. Debra continues to wonder what her organization and boss would like for her to do. Mark's company communicated these requirements, though he did not heed them. Debra's company has not made them explicit. Joan struggled to understand what her organization and bosses would allow women to do. She feels her misreading of the gender "rules" prevented her from achieving her earlier goals.

Matters are doubly complex when the head giraffe's requirements differ from those of the organization. Debra's team leader's desire for intimacy is more personal than organizational in nature. Mark isn't sure if the comfort requirements for promotion are those of the organization or his bosses. It's an important issue, because it will suggest how much trust he can put in the promotional process.

What is behind this common elephant dilemma? A key difficulty is that managers often don't communicate their own or the company's requirements clearly. Often managers are simply poor communicators, and to make matters worse, are at a complete loss with people who are different from themselves. Aspiring giraffes are able to intuit the requirements for success more rapidly than elephants; they've had more practice in reading the cues.

How do elephants go about determining the organization's requirements? They must use all available tools for gathering data: written materials, conversations, and observations of behavior. And they must not take information at face value. Their task is to find truth and reality by resolving any incongruencies.

They should not assume that lack of face validity means some-one is trying to sabotage their success. They should instead dig more deeply to find consistencies from which requirements can be gleaned.

Getting Comfortable With the Choices

Even elephants who understand the requirements and make de-cisions about them can have difficulty remaining comfortable with their decisions. Racial, ethnic, and gender elephants, for example, are likely to experience a negative response from their elephant peers. African Americans are sometimes accused of selling out in pursuit of organizational success. Women are asked pointed questions about child care arrangements. Gays and lesbians are chided for too much or too little disclosure of their sexual preference.

Matters are more complex because the assimilation rules have changed over the past two decades. Attitudes and actions once considered essential can be subjected to scorn. Older ele-phants in prominent positions can feel cast aside as younger ele-phants ignore their advice or deride their assimilation decisions.

Ray, Richard, and Carol demonstrate this delicate dilemma. Ray's position on affirmative action has created friction between his Mexican American co-workers and him. To date, he has not changed his mind, but he is aware of their disapproval. And as he advances further, pressure from this credibility gap is likely to grow. Richard's pressure comes not from his peers but from his sense of obligation toward the struggles of African Ameri-cans and gays and lesbians. His is an internal need to be credible. Carol has become aware of the limits and potential costs of wholesale assimilation.

Putting Extraneous Agendas in Perspective

Elephants who adopt extraneous agendas are less likely to be-come effective diversity respondents or achieve organizational success than those who skirt this hindrance. Ultimately busi-nesses exist to make a profit. Anything that does not affect the bottom line is extra. Elephants forget this at their peril. That is why diversity management's agenda does not explicitly advocate a social agenda. Instead, it focuses on achieving organizational objectives and accessing talent toward that end.

Diversity management does not, for example, advocate gay rights or women's rights. It does not call for reparations to African Americans for slavery. It calls for accessing talent regardless of sexual orientation, or gender, or race, as long as doing so does not compromise organizational requirements.

Confusion typically flows from the concepts of celebrating and valuing differences. Diversity management calls for neither. It requires instead that differences that don't conflict with organizational requirements be recognized, accepted, and understood. It does not require that any difference or attribute be valued or celebrated.

This is not to suggest that elephants should abandon causes that are important to them, only that they must assign them to the appropriate organizational agenda. Elephants who want their companies to support their agendas must find ways to fit them within the company's mission and priorities. Unless they can do so, they are unlikely to get their organization's support.

For-profit corporations do not exist to promote social agendas. Elephants who don't understand this are destined to be frustrated. Richard has experienced this frustration. So intense is his desire to eliminate bias and discrimination against African Americans and gays and lesbians that he has made it a significant personal requirement. He is often disappointed with the results. It is hard for him to understand that his causes are extraneous to his company's core purpose.

To reduce his disappointment, Richard has two courses of action. He can identify volunteer opportunities and other outlets that allow him to advance his causes. He can communicate to his managers the business motive—or bottom-line benefits—of an inclusive workforce and a managing diversity environment. It is the language of profits, not of causes, that is most likely to be heard.

Playing the Elephant Card

Nothing complicates the diversity maturity process for elephants more than elephants from "protected" groups playing the "ism" card. They play this card when they see their elephant status as the controlling factor in a situation. They say, in effect, "Because I am an elephant in a giraffe's house, I am being penalized."

Elephants who take this stand can expect "push-back." Many in the United States are convinced that the isms are a thing of the past. They believe this country has done all that it can for victims of discrimination. They don't want to hear about any remaining problems.

So when should an elephant play the elephant card? The answer is, It depends on whether the situation is private or public. The rules change according to the setting.

When reflecting on their situation, it's reasonable for elephants to expect difficulties in a giraffe's house. Indeed, these difficulties can be best understood when viewed from an elephant's reality. Thus elephants should keep this card readily available for use in personal reflection and analysis—for example, in developing strategies that enhance the elephant's effectiveness while in the giraffe's house. When looking for reasons for and solutions to problems, overemphasis on the elephant card is foolhardy. But so is a refusal to consider the possibility that an ism is at work.

Using the card in public is more complex. Elephants should not hesitate to play the card in public when it reflects the reality they are experiencing and can contribute to the likelihood of progress. This clearly is a judgment call, and elephants who do so should be prepared for a strong reaction. Both individuals and organizations withhold sympathy or empathy from those claiming victim status. Giraffes often experience the use of this card as an accusation of them and an attack on their character. Giraffes receive accusations of discrimination poorly.

In both private and public settings, caution is in order. Elephants who automatically assume an ism or prejudice on the part of others or believe that all unsatisfactory experiences are the consequence of their elephant status are ultimately self-defeating.

Dealing With Rage

The vigor and success with which giraffes refute such charges give rise to another hindrance to elephants becoming effective diversity respondents. It encourages or refuels rage that is all too real to the elephant but seen as illegitimate by others.

Rage surfaces wherever the concerns and needs of elephants remain unaddressed or unresolved. It is particularly likely where individual giraffes (legitimately or not) disclaim responsibility for the issues that offend.

What do elephants do with rage that others refuse to recognize or endorse? There is no formula. Rather, several strategies are successful. Coping elephants frequently use denial or suppression. Denying elephants minimize the importance of the source of the rage, thus reducing the amount of attention the situation requires. Suppressing elephants allow the rage-producing conditions and the rage to slip from their mind. Another coping option is to withdraw emotional investment from the organization by lowering expectations.

Debra and Richard demonstrate coping mechanisms. Debra suppresses her rage, primarily because her family responsibilities require that response. It is not clear that she will continue to do so. Richard currently copes with his rage by giving a priority to his causes, thus channeling his rage into constructive efforts. Mark responds to his rage by threatening to quit.

Accepting the rage as legitimate and owning it can be major steps forward. Some elephants find this difficult to do. Yet the worst option is not to address the issue at all. The damage to emotional and physical health can be serious.

FACILITATORS FOR MEETING THE CHALLENGES

Taking Charge

The most essential move that elephants can make toward becoming effective diversity respondents is to take charge of managing their own situation. They must accept responsibility for their decisions about requirements even when they believe they have little control.

Granted, this is difficult. It's far easier for elephants to blame their organization or supervisor for inept diversity management and to focus on ways in which the work environment does not empower them. It's discouraging to believe that they lack necessary diversity knowledge and skills. And it's tempting to see themselves as victims.

Indeed, these responses are common among elephants in all kinds of situations, not only those related to ethnicity, race, or gender. Senior managers operating in a new parent company as a result of an acquisition, for instance, experience all of these reactions. They can feel disempowered, unknowledgeable, and victimized by their reduced status.

Accepting Pioneer Status

Much more helpful—and exhilarating—is for elephants to see themselves as pioneers. The pioneering mind-set is empowering; people who know they are pioneering can prepare for it. If you expect to encounter a bear, you can equip yourself for the experience, but an unexpected encounter with the animal is likely to be traumatic.

Many elephants have not prepared for pioneering. Sometimes this represents nothing more than a lack of experience; they simply don't know what to expect. For others, however, it demonstrates unrealistic expectations. Recently a young elephant discussed his concerns about a move he planned to make: "What can I do to get some guarantees about the outcome of the move?" He was distressed to be told that there are no guarantees. Risks and more risks are the lot of pioneers.

Perhaps the most dangerous time for pioneering elephants is after they have achieved some organizational success. As they gain authority, responsibility, and status, they forget that there are still bears out there. As Joan discovered, forgetting can be dangerous. Pioneering elephants can never relax. Dangers at the top are no less than at the lower levels. It's still a giraffe's house.

How do elephants cope with the challenges of pioneering? They take a critical first step by recognizing that they are pioneers. (All elephants are not pioneers, nor are all pioneers elephants.) Race, gender, ethnicity, and sexual orientation come to mind, but other examples exist. If, for example, a corporation that routinely promotes from within decides to hire experienced professionals, these professionals become pioneers. Many of the old assumptions won't work for them. They will be intensely scrutinized, and they are likely to experience extra stress.

Pioneering elephants should network with other pioneers within and outside their organization. They should exchange experiences and learnings, and reaffirm each other's value as persons, professionals, and pioneers. This sounds straightforward, but often it is not. Elephants who want to assimilate and convince others that they can do so see little benefit in an elephant network.

Finding a Mentor

The experiences of Joan, Debra, Mark, and Ray suggest that mentors can be key to helping elephants address diversity effectively.

The most effective mentoring relationships probably occur naturally. However, elephants should feel free to recruit mentors, as Debra did, when none volunteers. They should, in fact, seek different mentors for specific purposes because one person is unlikely to be able to give all the guidance needed.

Developing Mature Attitudes

Diversity maturity is largely a matter of mind-set. Elephants striving toward diversity effectiveness will do well to attend to these attitudes:

Accept diversity, even when it's unpleasant. This means, for example, that gays and lesbians can work toward a common objective with a co-worker who rejects them, African Americans can work alongside racists, and women can work alongside male chauvinists, all in pursuit of a common objective. While in the workplace, their priority is to achieve organizational goals, not stamp out their co-workers' idiosyncratic isms. This does not mean accepting unacceptable behavior; it simply means being willing to accord other objectives a higher priority, within defined limits.

See the big picture. This gives elephants a perspective and context that allows them to look beyond themselves. It also creates a commonality with those who would otherwise be experienced as very different.

Focus on the moment. Diversity-mature elephants focus on the realities of the moment, not issues of the past. The task is not to ignore the past, but to keep it from distracting your efforts to meet current diversity challenges.

🐘 🐘 🐘

Clearly elephants face some challenges that giraffes do not. We never said it was going to be easy. Elephants can be excused for thinking that they bear a disproportionate share of the burden of making diversity work.

But make it work they can. Indeed, they must if they are to enjoy maximum personal and professional success. Elephants with the courage to become pioneers, the tenacity to work through the inevitable challenges and tensions associated with elephant status, and the skills and imagination to craft mutual adaptation solutions can do more than ensure their personal success. They can move their organizations in the direction of diversity effectiveness too.

PART FOUR
Giraffes in Action

GIRAFFES are the insiders. They define what "normal" is and establish the rules accordingly. They are in control either formally or informally. It is their house.

As with the elephant, neither race, gender, nor ethnicity necessarily or even primarily determines the giraffe status. At its core is the assignment or assumption of house ownership. We all can—and do—play both the giraffe and elephant role at different times in different settings.

To understand giraffe status fully, think back to your childhood. Many of us first recognized and came to terms with "owners" on the playground. They were the kids who dictated what games would be played and the relative rank of all the players. Maybe they had this status because they were very skilled at the game, or perhaps because they owned the ball. In school, the "owners" determined what was cool. However *cool* was defined, those who met the definition were granted giraffe status.

These early experiences give many a glimpse of what will prove to be a lifelong experience: being a giraffe, or living and working among them.

◄ Race, gender, and ethnicity can and frequently do determine giraffe status, and in business organizations, the main giraffes are often white men. But that is by no means the full story. Many other factors determine giraffe status.

◁ *Legacy*. People whose predecessors (family members or others with whom they are historically connected) served as giraffes sometimes believe they have the right to pick up the mantle.

◁ *Excellence*. In some settings those who excel gain giraffe status. Michael Jordan's excellence on the basketball court gives him giraffe status. Yet excellence cuts both ways. Academic excellence in high schools, for example, can sometimes confer elephant, not giraffe, status.

◁ *Legal ownership*. The legal owners of the company usually have de facto giraffe status.

◁ *Fulfillment of norms*. Those who meet giraffe-established norms are granted giraffe status. If people in a company believe that Building 52 is where the action and power are, those who work there become giraffes. If giraffe norms call for a valuing of those who are tall, lean, and athletic, those fitting this description are considered to be giraffes.

Neither giraffe nor elephant status is immutable. People can be giraffes in one setting and elephants in another. Many factors have a mirror-imaging dynamic. If the lack of a degree from a prestige school makes you an elephant, for example, then having this degree makes you a giraffe. If not being a member of a preferred function confers elephant status, being a member confers giraffe status.

Being a giraffe allows you to avoid the challenge of being in another's house. But it doesn't guarantee a positive experience, particularly when the giraffe status was conferred, not earned.

🦒 *10* 🦒

The Assimilated Giraffe: George

George's Story

I'm a white male who has been at this organization for twenty-some years. Before coming here, I had graduated from college with a degree in accounting, served in the Vietnam War, and worked for two large corporations and the federal government.

I was one of the original members of this organization. I started off as an accountant, then spent five years as a corporate internal auditor. I spent the next eleven years in various positions. About three years ago, I moved over to customer service. I've been a third-level manager for two or so years. There are 150 people in my organization. Eight are direct reports.

The Company

This is a company that values integrity and consistency. To be successful here, you have to embrace the organization's way fully. You have to live it, to be true to it. You also have to be steady in your performance, to stay even-keeled. These things I am. Someone once said of me, "Whatever else you might say about him, he's consistent." I don't think I am much different today than I was the day I walked into the organization.

Managerial success in this company also requires very good people skills. This company believes that if everybody knows what he or she has to do, and if managers give people the right

155

resources and treat them like human beings, they'll do a superior job. Managers must be able to motivate their subordinates to go to that next level of effort to be successful.

I think my background helped me to acquire these skills. I've lived all over the United States and in Europe. We moved every three years or so when I was young, so I was always having to adjust. I was attached to a large government agency in Washington, D.C., for several months. That's where I got over the fear of speaking and learned to think on my feet in front of a large audience.

Challenges and Disappointments

If I have a disappointment with the organization, it's the slowness with which it is becoming more diverse. I see evidence that the company is trying. Recently we had an intense week dedicated to activities that focused on diversity. Workshop participants included African Americans, Asian Americans, whites, Native Americans, and Hispanics, males and females, and gays and lesbians. Our facilitators had that same kind of mix. They focused on getting the groups together.

Some people really saw it as a slap in the face. I thought it was quite healthy for my fellow managers who I knew really needed training. But I think it was a reminder to me of the world we live in, and it really pumped me up to see my organization making efforts to address diversity in general.

I feel strongly about the issue. To me, diversity means no barriers. It means we're all the same. It means it doesn't matter. It means I will respect you as an individual. It means you will be given the same opportunity as anyone else. It means I'd like to change the world, but I don't know what to do.

I see the challenges that nonwhite male employees have to face in the company. I believe that people doing the same jobs are paid commensurately. We've also made some movement in the area of higher-level job opportunities for females. You can't go past age sixty at this organization and be a vice president. A few years ago, the company made a special effort to put some women in positions to replace retiring VPs.

Minorities haven't fared as well. Not too long ago, a personnel representative told me he was having difficulty scratching out enough minority numbers to ensure that the organization wouldn't look like the Ku Klux Klan. I think that's because our president and VPs have always been white folks, and they're always going to be white males. In addition, there's always been a good old boys network that sort of ran the southeast division. It wasn't until the company changed presidents a few years ago that they even realized they weren't with the program. This situation doesn't make me happy. I would prefer if my mix of employees were different.

Sometimes a bold move does result in real progress. Our visionary vice president sought the most qualified minorities he could for the general manager's job here. And he had to go far north and probably made this man an offer he couldn't refuse to come to this southern city. I'm not sure my friends were comfortable with that. As a result of the VP's initiative, I work for an Asian American man. I thought it was the neatest thing that ever happened, actually, and I have been absolutely pleased.

I've been a broken record on diversity for years. For years I was dissatisfied that we weren't actively recruiting and hiring minority candidates for higher-level jobs. I do think that is changing, but we still like to make our numbers at the lowest level.

Personal Diversity Background

My views about diversity were formed on the military bases where I lived when I was young. I grew up in a completely diverse environment. I had never experienced segregation. The shock of my life came in 1961 when I was in the ninth grade. We were living in this little microcosm—a bomber base in the north of England. My best buddy was black. We were inseparable. My dad sat me down and told me we had been transferred to the southern part of the United States. He also told me about segregation and what I was going into. My parents were very concerned about my well-being going into that segregated community. They had reason to be. I was in a southern high school when Martin Luther King, Jr., came to the front door. I was shocked by my classmates' responses to his presence.

What could I do? The locals didn't want to hear my views on

segregation. In fact, it would probably have been dangerous to try to share my convictions. I had to withdraw. I had to live as a multiple personality at the time to survive in that community.

Dealing With Differences

There are some differences that I struggle with, but I think I understand that people are the sum result of their lives. If you live in poverty and you get less than an average education; if you have less than a normal family environment, whatever normal is these days; if you're raised with just one parent; if you don't know where your next meal is coming from and no one cares if you excel in school, and you live in an environment that is less than wholesome, your attitudes on life are going to be different than mine.

You could also live in an environment that is everything that mine is. But if your culture or your religion is different, your attitude about life is going to be different from mine. That different point of view can help you to be successful.

The people who do drive my blood pressure up are those who say things without thinking them through. I pay attention to details, and I don't rush into decisions. When I have an important issue, I sit on it. I do my best thinking in gridlock. I don't like sloppy thinking. When I say I want a good mix of people, I still want these people to pay a great deal of attention to detail.

Making a Difference

I often ask myself, Within this organizational setting, what could I have done to make more of a difference? I've never minced words with folks about needing to have more diversity. Why aren't we doing more?

I've tried to do my part, and I've had some real good success cases with black males. A former boss told me, "You can't hire those people. They're on drugs." I ignored him and hired a veteran. (I have a soft spot for vets.) This guy had been a bartender. I hired him for the most menial job. Then I gave him an old PC. He taught himself to use it, then went on and put himself through college.

Now he's very successful. He just got a big promotion. The first thing I did when I heard was to go give him a big hug and pat him on the back. I can walk around the building and see people I've hired over the years in entry-level jobs and see them be successful. If I've had any measure of success, that's it. When I've had the opportunity to contribute to the diversity of this organization, I've taken it.

Still, it has been in only the past two or three years that I think I've had some power from which to address diversity at higher organizational levels. I know what I want to do, but I'm in a box.

It's almost unheard of for someone to hire a manager from outside the organization. Once in a great while, someone will get really desperate and hire a supervisor from the outside. But usually people start off at the lowest level or as an individual technical contributor. We don't have a good supply of internal minority candidates who are being developed for the next step, and we don't do a good job of retaining the ones we are lucky enough to get.

A while ago, I had openings for two good jobs with good relocation packages. I needed two people—one with specific skills, the other with more general skills. I had to rely on my human resources people because these are internal postings. I didn't get a black candidate.

Now once more I have a job, and once more there's no way that this job is going to be filled from the outside. I have no pool of diverse talent within the organization from which to draw. I find that frustrating.

GEORGE AS SKILLED DIVERSITY RESPONDENT

George is disappointed with his organization's progress in recruiting and promoting minorities. He has pondered whether he has done all that he could do to change this situation. Still, he is largely content with his contributions. He notes that his background predisposed him to work in a diverse workforce environment. And he reports that he has had success with black males.

George reports that unlike his peers, he welcomed the recruitment of a qualified minority for his boss's position, and he says that he has no difficulty at all working for a minority male.

George's Diversity Maturity

Accepts Responsibility

George is sincerely committed to diversity (as he defines it) but does not include himself in the mix. He is proud of the company's recent diversity training, but thinks it is others who need it, not him. He would like to increase the diversity among the workforce (again, as he defines it) but believes he is hampered by company policies. In short, George places responsibility for his company's diversity shortcomings on corporate policies and other people. Any problems, he believes, are the result of decisions over which he has no control.

Demonstrates Contextual Knowledge

An Understanding of the Organization. George understands the rules for success in his organization: "You have to fully embrace the organization's way." He not only embraces the organization's way; as one of the original members in this regional facility, he has had a hand in shaping it. For the most part, he is happy with both the organization and his position in it.

The Business Motive. Because of his strong commitment to following the company way, George will be most likely to embrace genuine diversity if he can identify how this will benefit the company. He can do so by connecting with his company's current environmental realities and determining where flexibility, nimbleness, and creativity are needed. He may well discover, for instance, that the company needs people who are original thinkers more than it needs people who are good at details. George should encourage his managers to consider the same questions. He is far more likely to get organizational support for the diversity that he seeks if it becomes clear that business viability is at stake.

Conceptual Clarity About Diversity. George is as yet unac-
quainted with genuine diversity. Like a great many other people, he equates diversity with representation, with inclusion.
When he says, "When I've had the opportunity to enhance the
diversity of this organization, I've taken it," he means that he
has hired people who represent different demographics.

This understanding of diversity has led him to focus on affirmative action approaches. This approach assumes that white
men are the norm; all others are different. It also assumes that
those who are included will leave their differences at the door.
It thus unwittingly discourages the diversity that its proponents
report that they seek.

Is Clear About Requirements

Committed organization men can find it difficult to distinguish between their company's preferences, conveniences, and
traditions on the one hand, and its genuine requirements on the
other. They tend to assume instead that if organizational leaders
prefer a course of action, it is by definition a requirement. This
leaves little or no room for genuine diversity.

"When I say I want a good mix of people," George is quick
to point out, "I still want these people to pay a great deal of
attention to detail." He defines this attentiveness as a required
competency.

George does have some sense that he is caught in this conceptual trap. He would like to fill two attractive openings with
"diverse" workers, but finds no qualified black candidates from
inside the company and is prohibited from searching outside.
He doesn't like it, but he goes along with this precedent. He
seems not to consider bucking the policy, as did an admired vice
president. At issue isn't whether he was right or wrong in this
particular instance. It is his assumption that he had no creative
choices. Company policy prevails.

Places Differences in Context

George's belief that others are responsible for the lack of
adequate representation leads him to see the diversity issue as

outside of himself, and that has prevented him from examining his own views concerning people who are different.

George experienced the preintegration South and identified with the struggle of minorities for inclusion. He sees diversity as a social responsibility issue—something he and his organization must work toward for the benefit of others. Yet he seems unaware that he equates differences and elephant status with deficiencies. He speaks with compassion of those who had a "less-than-normal family life, less-than-average education" but believes that this "less than" background is what makes them different.

If challenged on this point, George would undoubtedly deny that he thinks people who are different are in some way deficient, because that would conflict with his values. But in denying this reality, he makes his beliefs about differences inaccessible to himself (although they are probably visible to others) and to possible change.

George's belief that diversity is a social responsibility issue and his preference for assimilation also keep him from assessing differences in light of the effect their inclusion will have on the organization. He assumes that those with different attributes will conform to company ways once they gain entry into the organization.

Core Diversity Skills

◀ *Ability to identify diversity mixtures.* George focuses on one key diversity mix: demographic characteristics. He identifies race, gender, ethnicity, religion, and sexual orientation as significant diversity dimensions. He implicitly identifies social class as a significant mix as well but does so in a way that leaves it intertwined with other primary diversity dimensions.

George is also affected by an additional mixture of which he is only vaguely aware: that of how he would like society and his organization to be, and the way he perceives that they are. This mixture creates an internal tension within George, leaving him feeling frustrated and disappointed.

◀ *Ability to analyze the mixtures and related tensions.* George does not routinely ask himself, "What is the most significant mixture and tension, given the business requirements?" He uses a personal yardstick instead to measure mixture importance. Key to his ability to move his organization in the direction he wants it to go is to begin identifying where addressing a diversity mixture and related tension will help his organization to solve a problem or take advantage of an opportunity.

◀ *Ability to select an appropriate response.* George prefers to include those who are demographically diverse (ensure representation). But he excludes behavioral diversity when choosing his own actions and determining which to accept from others. George's decision to embrace the organization's way is a decision to assimilate. Even though he is often frustrated by company policies, he acquiesces. Furthermore, he expects assimilation from employees, not only around organizational requirements but around preferences, traditions, and conveniences as well.

He acknowledges frustration but suppresses his feelings and remains on an even keel. When he watched classmates reject integration, he suppressed his feelings and acted in public as if nothing was wrong. When he is disappointed in his company or in an employee's performance, he suppresses and carries on. He expects others to do so too.

WHAT'S NEXT FOR GEORGE?

To grow as an effective diversity respondent, George must take a path that is different from the ones he is used to taking. He must become a pioneer. If he waits until the company endorses diversity before changing his behaviors, he will end up disappointed. He owes it to himself to try something different.

A significant first step would be to redefine what he means in using the word *diversity*. By limiting his definition to inclusion, George unduly hamstrings himself. He could also benefit from understanding the differences in the diversity approaches and their effectiveness in achieving specified goals. He is familiar with affirmative action and its representation goals. But now that he is in a position to affect company policy, he must learn more about diversity management. Managing diversity assumes that differences and similarities cross demographic lines. It also assumes that diverse people will behave as they feel and think within the context of meeting requirements.

To further his journey toward diversity maturity and attain the diversity goals that he champions, George should also do the following:

◀ *Test his assumptions and understandings.* To do this, he could establish relationships within and outside the company with people who disagree with his views. This will do more than provide access to insights and convictions that differ from his own. It will sharpen his understanding of his own suppositions and convictions as well.

◀ *Try out the principal diversity approaches in settings that matter to him.* This would give him a personal sense of the approaches' best uses and their pros and cons. This understanding would transform head knowledge into experiential knowledge and genuine understanding.

◀ *Stay in the learning mode.* George should reexamine his belief that he needs no additional training. The practice of managing diversity, in particular, is still in its early phase. No one can declare, "I need no more learning. I've seen and done it all." We are, in truth, just starting.

◀ *Seek out diversity role models who have successfully made a difference either within or outside the organization.* George knows of a man who successfully confronted the organization's culture and made both a statement and a difference.

George has genuinely sought diversity progress for years, but he has not achieved the hoped-for results, and he is feeling discouraged. He needs to take bold actions, starting by reexamining his assimilation assumptions. If he decides to move ahead in this way, George could be a powerful force in changing his organization.

11

The Uncompromising
Giraffe: Jeff

Jeff's Story

I've been with this organization for ten years. I'm forty-one years old. Things happened pretty late in life for me. I didn't graduate from college until I was twenty-nine. I didn't get this job until I was thirty-one. Before college, I bummed around. I tried to find myself in a lot of things. Going to college put me on track with computers, and I've been on it ever since.

I purposely sought out this company because everyone I talked to said it was a great company to work for, and it's true. It's like a family. It's more unlike a corporation than any other corporation I've worked for. This is a corporation that truly respects the employee and tries to do what is right. Management has traditionally been very open to working with its employees on just about any problems that they've had.

Success Defined

For me, success is providing for my family and doing something I enjoy. I haven't always defined it that way. Up until about three years ago, I wanted to be on the fast track. After working for the organization in California, where I met and married my wife, I came back to Birmingham in 1993.

The next year, 1994, was pivotal for me. I was flying more, spending more time out of town, more time in meetings, more time trying to manage the organization's strategic direction. My career was going very well. Then two things happened. The first was work-related. The second had to do with my family.

I had my first tough encounter with office politics that year. I was one of three people hired to build a support organization for a software program the company was launching. Our job was to build the organization. But we had very few staff, so we did a lot of the task-oriented work as well. I was amazed that people wanted their own way in dealing with certain areas of the business even though it meant delays in the software and not doing the right thing for the customer. For example, we had two women on the team who kept promoting ideas that weren't valid. I tried to say so. But I had a difficult time getting my point across, so I circumvented the problem instead of facing it head on.

The women went to my manager, and I received a severe reprimand on an evaluation. I was told I was not a team player. My customers loved me. They gave me the highest marks that you could get. But the team did not. That was an eye-opening experience. I said, "Okay, now I understand what it's all about. You have to play the political game and please the customer at the same time." I wasn't willing to do that, and that has blocked my success. I have no tolerance for politics. Politics is simply self-interest, and I didn't want to play the game.

The other big thing that happened was much worse. At the end of 1994, my dad got sick. Two months later he died—just like that. I had precious few months to spend with him because I had spent that whole year building my career. I'll never get those times back.

That opened my eyes, and I said, "Never again am I going to sacrifice my family for the fast track." That, plus not wanting to be in a situation where I'd have to play politics, led me to think about starting my own business. Now, three years later, I own my own company, and I also work here at this organization twenty to thirty hours a week. The job here is more technical. It allows me to come into the office to do what I've got to do and then go home. To me, this is success.

Views on Diversity

I think diversity is a very misunderstood concept. A lot of people don't have a clue about what it's all about. When I think about diversity, I think of how we should be all-inclusive. Specifically, I think of blacks and whites—skin color differences. Diversity is about including people of all races, nationalities, and both genders without their feeling excluded for any reason because of their appearance, the way that they were made by God.

It's about leveling the playing field, making equal opportunities for everyone. But I think we have to look very carefully at how it's done and to realize that if you start promoting diversity by saying, "We're going to include this group," that also means you're not going to include other groups. Myself being a white male, a born-again believer in Christ, for example, I feel as if I'm a minority now because that's the way the political climate is going.

My beliefs about diversity are shaped by my background and my religion. I'm a southerner by birth. I'm proud to be a southerner, but I've seen the way blacks are treated in the South, and I think it is totally wrong. A person should never be made to feel inferior simply based on skin color.

But behavior is another thing, and that's where I think that we need to define diversity clearly. If diversity is behavior, then I can say, for example, "I'm a Nazi; why can't you include me if you're doing diversity?" Well, why not? If you're going to include this group over here that behaves a certain way, why not include this other group that behaves a certain way? You have to draw your lines based on what I believe the Bible talks about with morality: what is moral, what is upright, what will benefit society. That's where I am with diversity.

I have been a Christian for fifteen years now, and that's what molds and shapes every aspect of my life. I'm also part of the Promise Keepers. I think they are doing the best thing in the world in reconciling the differences between blacks, whites, Hispanics. At one event, I ended up hugging this sixty-year-old black man and saying, "I'm sorry for what my forefathers did." I think we need to come to a reconciliation of that. The only way we're ever going to get anywhere is to be able to love one another as Christ loves us. There shouldn't be any judgment between any of us.

Taking a Stand

About a year and a half ago people in this organization decided that diversity meant basically a coming-out party. *Diversity* became a buzzword for the gay lifestyle. I would sit in the cafeteria and see the little banner things they had on the table. The very first item under diversity was inclusion of homosexuality. At one point, gay and lesbian parties were being announced on the blue monitors in the lobby where customer notices should be. The organization also helped sponsor the Gay Pride Parade, and some of our managers carried signs linking our organization and products with their gay lifestyle. The result was that a lot of people got turned off by diversity.

I couldn't accept that, so I went directly to the general manager. I knew we would disagree, and I thought, "This could very well end up getting me out of the company." But amazingly enough, he was very open to talking to me about the situation. In fact, I really think he understands diversity just about better than anyone else I talk to.

After I talked to him, I went to the company's president and CEO, the corporate diversity manager, and several other managers. I even went to the vice president of the entire organization.

This man didn't have a clue. He really thought that diversity meant that we, the white oppressor, had to give everything away to everyone else. That meant that there is nothing you could be that wouldn't be all right because that's the only way to make the past right. I said, "I'm sorry; I disagree," and he and I got into a yelling match.

That's when I decided I had to do something more, not just avoid the issue, as I had with those two women on the software project. So I got people together. Several of us stood in front of a room with thirty high-level managers. We said, "This is not about diversity. This is about someone who wants to promote their personal agenda, and I don't think this organization should be a part of promoting or sponsoring that." From that time, I thank the Lord, we haven't heard anything else from the gay and lesbian community.

Consequences of the Protest

The protest has been a growing experience for me. Christians have a tendency to be very narrow-minded in some areas and focus in on the negative dos and don'ts instead of being inclusive and loving. That's what I think I have learned in the past year as we've gone through this homosexual movement and things like that.

When I began my protest, I didn't care what other people thought of me. I know some people respected me for it. Other people thought I was a fool. As time goes by, I'm glad that I did it. It has been a good experience for me. I gained a deep respect for my general manager, and I learned something about being honest and sticking to my beliefs.

I also got to see a different lifestyle. I'm able to look into the heart and minds of these people now. I am seeing them differently. God helped me to do this. I couldn't have done it without him because I learned to have compassion for something that I hated. I still hate the lifestyle, but I don't hate the people. I understand, and I love the people.

This was brought home to me one day when I was sitting in the cafeteria with friends. This skinny, skinny, skinny black man came and sat down, and it was like God pointed him out to me, and I looked at him and saw the soul of the man. He was homosexual, no doubt about it, and I think he had AIDS. I had such a compassion for him, because I saw exactly what was happening.

Here was a man whom God loved whose lifestyle, which is inspired by Satan, was trying to kill him. It was doing a darn good job of it, because this guy was pitiful. He could barely lift his fork to eat. I'm sure he was dying. At that point I realized that this is not about people—flesh and blood. This is something deeper, and these people are victims of what is going on in society right now. I saw into the heart of these people, and it's very sad. I felt a deep compassion for them. God revealed that to me. I could never have seen it on my own.

I dealt with a battle that I never expected to deal with. I'm glad I did because it opened my eyes. In addition, standing up for something, no matter what it is, is a liberating feeling. I feel that I've had a part to play in the direction that diversity has taken here in this organization and throughout the company.

New Directions

I'm using what I learned about being direct and open in running my own business. I know there are certain things you don't tell your people. But when they have a need to know, you should tell them. If there is a lack of understanding, you should explain it to them. If there is a difference of opinion, you should allow them to state their opinion. But at the same time, the end objective has to be maintained, so you have to move forward with whatever decision you've made. If people aren't on board with that, then they should leave. I don't think we should play political games because for one reason or another you're afraid to tell people something.

We've lost people at my own company because of this. But I believe we have a better organization now as a result. We have weeded out those who will work with this directness from those who won't.

It's very difficult to build a business from scratch when there is such a labor shortage. I'm looking for skilled people who want to stay with me to build the core of the business. I've had several people come and go. I have had people who understood that theirs was not a nine-to-five job, and that has been very rewarding. I wish they had stayed longer.

I only had one guy who has stayed with me through this start-up process of building the business. He sees it the way I do. You really have to pay your dues and put in your time to make it happen. He's a full partner in the business now. I feel good about him being there.

Everyone who left gave me fair notice except for one who, incidentally, was a woman. She was a very talented individual, and I enjoyed working with her. But her big thing was kids and all this. She didn't give me any warning. She just left. But what do you do? Start looking for somewhere else. That's just life, I guess.

JEFF AS EFFECTIVE DIVERSITY RESPONDENT

In most organizations, Jeff's unwillingness to tolerate circumstances that are not to his liking would result in an elephant (minority) status. His unwillingness to participate in office politics would make him even more of an outsider. It is only in his own business where he serves as head giraffe that he can insist on congruency with his thinking. As the owner of the company, this is his prerogative. Whether it is wise is another matter.

Jeff's Diversity Maturity

Accepts Responsibility

Jeff isn't interested in promoting diversity. His understanding of diversity and his responsibility for it are narrow, and he wants to leave it that way. Step one in achieving status as an effective diversity respondent is a desire to do so.

Demonstrates Contextual Knowledge

An Understanding of Self. Jeff has two significant qualities found in diversity mature individuals. He is aware of his beliefs and feelings, and he "owns" them. He is willing to stand up for what he believes. He has the tenacity needed to become an effective diversity respondent, should he decide to do so. Were he to take this critical step, several additional steps would be needed. Key would be gaining clarity on the distinction between representation and diversity. All other activities rely on this.

Conceptual Clarity About Diversity. When Jeff says *diversity*, he means representation or inclusion, and he limits representation to just a few dimensions: skin color, race, nationality, and gender.

Jeff bases his decision as to whether a dimension should be included on his understanding of the Bible. He excludes dimensions that he perceives as acts of will, and since he believes that homosexuality is a personal choice, he does not think it warrants being included as a diversity dimension. He includes white males in the diversity mix. He fears that efforts to include one group can work to exclude another, and believes this is happening with white males. He reports feeling like a minority. Implicit in Jeff's comments is a belief that diversity is a zero-sum game. He speaks as if to include one group is to exclude another automatically.

Is Clear About Requirements

Clarity about the difference between preferences and requirements is particularly important if Jeff is to succeed in running his own business. Here he needs to think about his own motives: is he insisting on assimilation because the business needs everyone to act and think the same, or because it makes him more comfortable?

In a workplace setting, attention to business requirements is the best foundation for diversity decisions. If Jeff persists in hiring and retaining only those who see it the way he does, he will limit himself to one mold, and that one mold may not be the best way to build his business. To close out diversity is to stifle creativity and nimbleness at a time when both are essential to organizational survival.

Jeff should ask himself the following questions before bringing an employee on board:

- ◀ Am I willing to include this person?
- ◀ Does he or she have any beliefs, characteristics, or requirements that make me uncomfortable?
- ◀ Am I willing to allow this person to demonstrate those characteristics or meet these requirements so long as they don't interfere with his or her ability to do the work?

If the answer to the last question is no, Jeff may want to defer the hiring. It is unlikely that talented employees in a tight job market will agree to remain in a "my way or the highway" environment.

He may also want to explore the wisdom of basing his opinions and decisions about diversity primarily on the dictates of his religion and personal preferences, as opposed to requirements. For Jeff, this caution has multiple implications.

In his work at the large organization, he has a history of basing his actions on preferences. He led an effort to change the company's initiatives on behalf of the gay community because he felt the company was promoting a social agenda that he found distasteful. And he declined to invest time and energy in working out his differences with the two women on the project team because he didn't want to "play politics."

Jeff was probably correct in his belief that his company's efforts on behalf of gays and lesbians exceeded those related to business requirements. His managers appear to have acknowledged this when they backed off from their decisions. It seems clear, however, that he was driven by his own sense of morals, not an analysis of business requirements. And clearly he erred in ignoring the requirement for teamwork when he disagreed with his women teammates.

Places Differences in Context

Finally, Jeff would benefit from greater sophistication around differences. He now is open to hiring and including people with differences he does not value, as long as they leave them at the door. If these individuals—in a Dennis Rodman fashion—insist on having their differences acknowledged and respected, Jeff may be unable to comply. He likely would view respecting the difference as tantamount to valuing or supporting it.

Jeff would be wise to develop the capability to understand the differences and similarities among respecting, accepting, conditionally accepting, and valuing differences, and to determine under what conditions each response would foster organizational growth. His "leave it at the door" stance is unlikely to work in either his own business or in the organization where he continues to work.

Core Diversity Skills

◀ *Ability to identify diversity mixtures.* Jeff has a narrow view of diversity. He sees it solely in terms of demographic mixtures and limits these to race, gender, and ethnicity. He has thought a great deal about sexual orientation, for one example, but believes it has no place in a "diversity" discussion. From his interview we see glimpses of other diversity mixtures that he does not see: the mixture of personal goals and work/life choices represented by his employees, the mixture of communication styles (not everyone shares his appreciation of directness), and the mixture of religious beliefs.

◀ *Ability to analyze the mixtures and related tensions.* There can be little doubt that the diversity mixtures, both acknowledged and unacknowledged, created major tensions in both the larger organization and Jeff's own company, and little doubt that Jeff was aware of these tensions. But he has not acquired the ability to look objectively at the situation and its tensions, assess them within the context of business requirements, and choose a course of action.

Consider the woman who left his company because of child care concerns. She was, by Jeff's account, an excellent employee, but she was unwilling to meet his "beyond nine-to-five" expectations. In relating the incident, he is most in touch with his annoyance that she did not give adequate notice. He fails to recognize that he played a part by not looking for ways to access her talents within the context of her work-family parameters.

◀ *Ability to select an appropriate response.* Jeff believes in inclusion around demographic differences. But he responds to ideas and beliefs with which he disagrees by excluding or isolating the other persons or himself. His clash with his women teammates is evidence of this. When his disagreement with them evoked an unsympathetic response, he circumvented the women and ignored their recommendations.

He endorses the inclusion of gay and lesbian employees and simultaneously suppresses his feelings about their lifestyle as long as they keep it quiet. In effect, he practices toleration. Jeff responds similarly to differences within his own business. He directly refutes ideas and behaviors he sees as undesirable, and demands assimilation. When employees do not surrender those undesired behaviors or ideas, he is willing to exclude them.

WHAT'S NEXT FOR JEFF?

Jeff's journey toward diversity maturity is destined to be long and stressful. But he and his business would gain much should he decide to take it. Diversity skills aren't necessary just for personal effectiveness. They are key to organizational viability as well.

𝄢 *12* 𝄢

The Pioneering Giraffe: Kirk

Kirk's Story

I'm an information technology (IT) manager. I manage a staff of twenty-two people who do technical computer support, largely by telephone. I came into the organization five years ago as an individual contributor, doing the same things as the people I manage today. I've been through a couple of levels of management and probably will go through a couple more before I'm done with the organization.

I've moved very fast, but I'm still not at the level that I can be. I don't think I've fulfilled my personal abilities yet. I expect to continue to grow and want to learn and gain. Within a large corporation, everybody needs to succeed, or stockholders aren't going to be happy. Especially where I am now, I need other people to succeed in order for me to be successful. If this whole team working with me now isn't growing and meeting new challenges, then my team is going to be seen as not being one of the better teams. This means I'll be seen as not one of the better people managers.

If anything were to hamper me from moving up now, it would be the organization. We just went through some changes, so we're trying to figure things out. Eventually I'll have to decide whether to move sideways, go somewhere else within the larger organization to continue that upward climb, or just hang on and wait a while.

I've been in this situation before. When I first decided to get into management, I was fairly new at this organization. There were people ahead of me by pecking order, and I didn't feel at the time that I was a top choice within the organization. The organization that I'm in is staffed predominantly by women. I was a young white male. My direct manager was a woman who was a couple of years older than I was. Her managers were older women. I felt as if they were thinking, "Maybe he's not ready." I just didn't see that I was the popular promotable choice.

To my surprise, I did get the promotion and have been promoted again since that time. I have, however, continued to be a minority in my area. In my first supervisory job I had one black male working for me. The rest of the staff were predominantly black women. Five years ago, telephone support was just becoming big, and the pay structure around it wasn't that high. We had problems getting white males into this area. They would come out of college and say, "I'm not going to answer telephones."

Within the past couple of years, we've seen a lot of that change. There are more careers inside and outside the organization that involve telephone support. In addition, the pay has increased, and the job has more status. As a result, the support organization has begun to integrate more and more as this increased opportunity and higher pay has attracted more men.

When I came into the group, I was the eleventh person hired into the telephone support organization. Now we have over eighty people doing it. We also have a much better mix. We probably have a better diversity mix within our support organization than others do.

Response to Diversity

Diversity to me is having different mixes of people within the organization. In the past, I thought diversity was black and white, and that was it. I still see black and white people as a mix. But as a manager, some of the bigger issues for me are the religious right and the gay population. People have a bigger problem getting over beliefs and morals than they do getting over skin color.

Having a mix means that people can bring something different to the table. To me, that is good. If I wanted one other opinion, I'd bring one other person in the room. That person would probably look just like me and have the same ideas as me. I'd have him or her there just to make me feel better. That's not my idea of having a team. In fact, when I go into a meeting, my job is to play the other side, no matter what it is. If you say I believe this, I'll ask, "But what about this?" I'm the devil's advocate. I think that's important.

My job as a manager is to encourage as many different ideas as I can, then try to mold those different ideas into one common agreement, because otherwise the corporation would go in ten different ways.

Diversity Background

During the early part of my career, I spent nearly six years in the military. That's where I learned to be comfortable working within a diverse environment. My first military assignment was in the Philippines, so I was thrown directly into a mix. There were two white men in a group of twelve. The rest were black men and women. We used to have some really interesting conversations.

I grew up in the Midwest, and that is not a diverse environment. In fact, the minority population in Iowa is less than 2 percent. I had no minority friends. It wasn't a matter of choice, just a lack of exposure. One of the men couldn't believe that. He argued that maybe I just didn't see minorities. But I would say, "No. The diversity just wasn't there."

I needed the exposure I got in the military. Without it, I would find it very tough to see diversity as a priority and to see what it brings. Those conversations were very important and helpful to me.

As it is, I'm involved in diversity activities within the community and this organization. I work with different diversity groups in the city. I'm also on the unit council here at work. I think I was picked for my first diversity council because I was a white male, and there weren't many other white males on the council.

At first, I didn't know much about the different people or the ideas and terminology. But as I got into it, I found it was a topic I was interested in and believed in. I think I add a lot of value now, and not just because I'm a white male.

Diversity's Ambiguities

Diversity Within the Family

I've struggled with diversity. I'm a conservative person. My wife, by her choice, stays home and works. We're out to church twice a week. How do I deal with people who don't fit into that environment? I think that what's key here is understanding that not everybody has to have the same ideas.

I have two sisters who are gay. One I knew about; the other one I just recently found out about. We grew up in a Catholic environment. My father flew to the other side of the country to say, ''No, you can't be.'' The rest of the family didn't go to that extreme, but we were upset. My response was to talk to my sister and then to agree that we won't discuss those issues because it's not productive. With certain core beliefs like that, you're not going to come to an understanding. I'm not going to say, ''I think it's right,'' and she's not going to say, ''You're right, I'll change.'' That's the way she is. I'm not going to hate a sister.

Diversity Within the Workplace

Within the work environment, I understand that people have different backgrounds, ideas, and moral beliefs than I do. It's not my job to be in somebody's personal life. What I need to see when I'm in the office is what they bring to this corporation—what their strengths and ideas are. That's how the organization values them as well. Whatever the difference, I try to have an understanding. When I don't, I try to cope with it.

I expect employees to do the same. I always tell them, ''I don't expect you to be friends with the person sitting next to you. But when you're here, you have to be comfortable enough with that person to ask him or her a question or to answer that person's questions.'' That works for most people. They're relieved that I don't expect them to be best friends and go out after work to socialize.

I have had people who don't get along, and that amazes me. But I guess it shouldn't. I've got kids who are twenty-one or twenty-two, and I've got people who are in their fifties. When you put them into the same mix, they have different ideals, different backgrounds, different families.

Personal Conflicts Around Diversity

I have another issue with diversity as well. That's the conflict between my personal desire to be promoted and my equal desire to see everybody else promoted. You always know that when you go up against somebody else—a woman or a black male, for example—if that person has equal abilities, it's a good bet that he or she is going to get the job because corporations need to promote diversity mixes. If you're a white male, you have to be better.

I understand these decisions. In fact, I make them. As a manager, when I have two equally promotable people—a black woman and a white man, for example—and my group is top-heavy with white men, I may go with the black female. That's because in these situations the question comes down to what the organization needs, based on the diversity mix it already has and the one needed to make it diverse. An organization of all white men—or all anything—is not good.

This focus on a good mix is a good thing for the organization, but it's not necessarily a good thing for me. What it means is that young white males aren't the popular promotable choice, regardless of whether they should be. That's not just my frustration. It's been the biggest frustration for a lot of white males in the 1990s.

A lot of white men have those conversations together. It's not a movement. But if there are three white men sitting someplace outside the corporation and they all happen to be in business, whether they're in the same company or a different company, they'll have these feelings. If somebody says something about diversity in their corporation, they'll have very similar thoughts and concerns.

The most troubling thing is that it feels as if the numbers are all that count. I know that's not true. Managers don't just count numbers. But from the personal side, there is a feeling that they do. And we're the high number. So those of us who aren't at the top yet feel as if there are too many of us up there now. We don't think we'll be the next one picked to move up.

Don't get me wrong. I think it's great when good, strong women make vice president. My mother is a very strong woman; she owns her own corporation. My father died when I was eight, and my mother worked as a waitress and went to school to become a nurse. I was cared for by male and female nurses when my mom was off to class. She didn't get married again until five years later, so she supported us kids for five years.

I didn't live in an inner-city ghetto; I lived in Iowa. And I'm sure a struggle in Iowa was a lot different from a struggle in an inner city. But it was a struggle nevertheless. I value those experiences because they made me strong. I also think that the part of me that enjoys seeing other diverse groups' success is the result of being part of that hard struggle.

Still, as happy as I am when diverse people succeed, I want to be promoted too. It bothers me to know that if I were to be promoted to vice president, nobody would notice. People get excited when another woman gets named vice president. They don't get excited when they see another white male made vice president, regardless of how good he is.

They also don't understand that white men may need to talk. What's really sad is that whenever white men meet as a group, people initially think "white male militia." Yet we have a black employees group and a gay employees group. Why don't we have a white men's group? That leaves white men feeling pretty unsupported. They don't feel as if anybody is looking out for them. They see numbers count on the other side. They see books about bringing diverse groups into the workplace and think, "Where's the support for bringing more white men into the workplace?"

It also bothers me that people seem unwilling to allow white men to hold on to some of the qualities that are characteristic of white men. Recently I had a conversation with a young single black woman. Much of what she said sounded as if it was coming from a young single black woman. And she was being critical. I told her, "I'm a white male from Iowa. It used to be that people asked you to change to look and act like white men. That's what brought this whole diversity movement on. I'm not going to do that to you, and I don't want you doing it to me."

I was reminded of the movie *The Color of Fear* and thought about the black men who were told to leave their backgrounds at home. It seems as if now white men are being asked to leave what makes them white men at the door. White men tend to be defensive; they tend to be very overpowering, strong. They fight and they argue because they want to win. That's probably why they're running a lot of corporations now. I have my share of these qualities. During an evaluation a few years ago, my manager said that I seemed defensive at times, as if you couldn't change my mind. I agreed that I had to work on those qualities if I wanted to be promoted, and I did.

But there's a lot of white male in me. I was one of seven kids. Of course, I'm defensive. Of course, I'm very argumentative. But now I was being asked to leave a lot of what made me me at the door.

Looking Ahead

This diversity thing is complex. But on balance, I feel that I've been pretty successful in the corporation, and I think others do too. And I haven't changed completely. I just have to figure out how to make who I am fit with what the organization wants. And I think I've had to fit a lot. If I can achieve the right mix between staying who I am and making that fit within the organization, I expect to continue to succeed.

KIRK AS SKILLED DIVERSITY RESPONDENT

Kirk has been successful in his corporation and expects to continue. He hopes that others will be successful too. Diversity advocates in his corporation no doubt see him as a white man who truly believes in diversity, who has his heart in the right place. His department claims to have one of the best diversity mixes in the organization. He serves on the company's diversity council and works with various diversity thrusts in the community.

Kirk appears to reflect the ideals that diversity champions hope to see in white men. And, in fact, he does reflect those ideals. But he struggles with himself and with the issues. He is less optimistic about his career than he would like to be, and he worries that the diversity he promotes will make it harder to achieve his personal goals.

Kirk is a pioneering giraffe—one of the first generation of white males to experience any significant competition from people who are different from them. He has courage. His feet are in the right place. But he is having difficulty getting his heart to follow. His ambiguity, the gap between his explicit and implicit comments, and his multiple concerns reflect neither duplicity nor lack of sincerity about his diversity efforts. They reflect, instead, the complexity of diversity and the difficulty of being a pioneer.

Kirk's Diversity Maturity

Kirk demonstrates considerable progress in achieving diversity maturity. He seems likely to make even more.

Accepts Responsibility

Kirk has clearly made a personal commitment to addressing diversity effectively, and he is working to help his organization do so as well.

Demonstrates Contextual Knowledge

An Understanding of Self. Kirk is aware of and acknowledges both his positive and negative feelings with respect to diversity. He knows how he feels and why he responds as he does. This self-awareness is critical to full diversity maturity.

Conceptual Clarity About Diversity. Kirk engages diversity as a topic and explores various schools of thought on the subject. This is done through his work on the diversity council and his community diversity efforts. Yet much of Kirk's reported ambivalence springs from conceptual confusion, fueled in part by his lack of a vocabulary to match his growing understanding. He often says *diversity* when he means *representation* or *inclusion*. He has, however, broadened his definition of which mixes should be included and redefined which are most significant.

It is in regard to beliefs and ideas that Kirk uses *diversity* accurately. He knows that increased representation can generate a greater variety of ideas, and that this can lead to competitive advantage. But he may err in assuming that a room full of people who look different will automatically lead to variety. It is quite possible to have people who look different and think the same, especially in organizations where assimilation is the rule. It is also possible to have people who look the same yet think differently. Kirk tends to stereotype, to assume that to look alike is to think alike. He is explicit about this when speaking of white men: "They fight and they argue because they want to win. That's probably why they're running lot of corporations now."

This statement reveals Kirk's stereotypical views of minorities and women, implying that since they are not running corporations, they must not possess these qualities. He knows better. He describes his mother as a strong woman who owns her own corporation.

Yet he may operate out of negative assumptions of which he is unaware. He assumes that when women or minorities get a promotion, it must be because they were given preference over white males. He acknowledges they were no doubt equally qualified, but he has difficulty in thinking that a minority or woman might have been better qualified. This stereotypical reasoning can lead him to see any promotion of minorities and women as being at his expense. Small wonder that he is concerned.

Kirk's understanding of white men as a diversity group is also multilayered. On one hand he explicitly defines white men as an identifiable group—one that could be part of a diversity mix. Yet on the other hand, implicitly he sees them as the norm and everyone else as diverse.

Kirk's ambiguity contributes much to his unease. To the extent that he sees white men as the norm, he is arguing for the benefit of everyone but his reference group. To do that seriously and in good faith, as Kirk has, is to begin to feel like a minority—not so much in terms of the numbers but with respect to the focus of the organization's culture. This is critical. Many minorities and women distrust corporate cultures developed by and for white males. Kirk feels similarly. He reports feeling like a minority and believing that the changes he advocates are not likely to benefit him.

Indeed, he sounds like a minority. His statements about white men could easily have been said by women or traditional racial or ethnic minority groups:

"We're not understood or supported."

"We're told to leave our differences at the door."

"Every other group can meet except us. When more than two of us talk in public, it is some kind of conspiracy."

"We have to be overqualified to get promotions. Now I have to be better when I go into the interview."

Some would say that Kirk's concerns are the product of an overactive imagination, given that white males still dominate the numbers and hold all the senior executive positions in his organization. But the nature of his concerns argues that this is not so. Kirk's concerns focus on proposed changes that don't include white males or explicitly spell out benefits for them. He believes that some group must be discriminated against. This time, he fears, it may be white men. Within that context, his uneasiness makes sense.

Is Clear About Requirements

Kirk is quite clear about requirements. He stresses requirements and competitive advantage as the basis for addressing diversity within the workplace. For example, he recognizes the strategic implications of diversity for teaming and innovation. This recognition drives his interest and work in the diversity arena. He also stresses requirements in his approach to his family. His personal convictions argue against his sisters' sexual orientation, but his requirement is to continue to love his sisters, so he accepts and tolerates them even while his values call for rejection.

Is Comfortable With Diversity Tension

Kirk's clarity around requirements gives him the courage to act on his convictions and the willingness to experience discomfort as a result. He demonstrates these qualities in his relationship with his sisters. He demonstrates it in advocating for diversity because it will benefit his company while worrying that it will work to his personal detriment.

Core Diversity Skills

◀ *Ability to identify diversity mixtures.* Kirk demonstrates skill in identifying diversity mixtures and in inferring the reasons for observed differences. He understands, for example, that individuals of differing ages and life responsibilities are likely to see the world differently. This is fortunate because he addresses diversity on an ongoing basis. Members of his workforce vary with respect to values, beliefs, race, gender, age, work/life, tenure, sexual orientation, and religion. Within his department, he is both a member of the dominant demographic group and management, and a numerical minority. As such, he simultaneously functions as a giraffe and an elephant.

Departmental diversity is another important mixture. Of particular interest to Kirk is relative status. The telephone support function now commands more respect, more career options, and greater pay than when Kirk joined the company.

Within his family, Kirk identifies a sexual orientation mixture; two of his sisters are lesbian. He treats this fact as he would a mixture at work: by focusing on requirements.

He experiences a significant intrapersonal mix consisting of his conflicting diversity views: his genuine belief that women and minorities should be included and his fear about what this can mean for him. He acknowledges the conflict. But he does not define it as a diversity mix.

 Ability to analyze the mixtures and related tensions. Kirk demonstrates skill in analyzing mixtures and related tensions, particularly in determining the impact of the tensions. He makes no assumption that the workplace environment should be tension-free and indicates that he is comfortable in disagreeing with others. But he also states that he won't tolerate diversity tension that compromises his employees' ability to get the work done.

 Ability to select an appropriate response. Kirk fosters mutual adaptation when he requires employees to develop a relationship that allows them to perform their work even though they may not be friends. He advocates the business motive for addressing diversity and makes it a priority or requirement. He calls for conformity in regard to requirements and toleration in other dimensions. This provides a basis for good diversity management.

As a member of the diversity council, he seeks assimilation when he calls for enhanced inclusiveness or representation (what he calls diversity).

With regard to his sisters' sexual orientation, he chooses to tolerate, accept, and include. He is not willing, he has concluded, to reject or hate his sisters although he disagrees with their orientation.

Kirk suppresses his own diversity tension around gender, sexual orientation, and race in two ways. He raises his felt concerns only with other white men, and he stays out of touch with (denies) those assumptions about minorities and women that would make him uncomfortable with himself.

WHAT'S NEXT FOR KIRK?

Kirk will continue to move forward in his diversity journey if he is able to:

 Clear up his conceptual confusion about the difference between inclusion or representation and diversity.

◀ Own, monitor, and assess his implicit understandings and challenge those that could hold him back. To fail to do so will be to sabotage his best efforts.

◀ Address his tendency to stereotype.

◀ Abandon suppression as his only option when addressing diversity tension and be willing to express his concerns and feelings to those who might have a different perspective. This will enable him to work through his issues, questions, and fears, not keep them largely hidden. It will also allow him to focus his efforts on making the workplace environment one that doesn't advantage or disadvantage any employee or group.

Kirk's past behavior suggests that he won't give up his efforts now, even though he is feeling stressed. He's likely to continue his pioneering role and to experience the frustration and ambiguity that come with it. He has the potential to become a very effective diversity respondent.

⟨ 13 ⟩

Diversity Effectiveness: The Challenges for Giraffes

Giraffes face the same diversity management tasks as elephants, but they view these tasks from a different angle. As a result, their experiences and perceptions both converge with and diverge from those of elephants. There is considerable overlap, but very real differences as well.

CHALLENGES TO GIRAFFES

Recognizing Diversity Mixtures

Those who can't recognize a diversity mixture can't address it. Yet giraffes can have great difficulty with this essential task. Partly this is a result of their insider perspective. If you see yourself as embodying the "right way" and assume that those aspiring to higher status will assimilate to your way, diversity discussions may be of little interest to you. Should someone not fit in, you may counsel them, as did the giraffe in Chapter 1, on how to conform to your way. But you're unlikely to view diversity and diversity mixtures as deserving of serious personal attention. As a result, giraffes with limited experience in an elephant role may not recognize diversity in either themselves or others, and they seldom feel the need to address it.

Not all giraffes have this difficulty. Those who have had significant elephant experiences can more easily see diversity and the need for diversity management. They know how it feels to be designated an outsider. They also understand how important it is to address giraffe-elephant mixtures effectively.

Kirk, the giraffe with the greatest progress toward diversity maturity, provides an excellent example. He has experienced elephant status as a male in a predominantly female work group, and his evolving competence with diversity can be traced back to his earlier elephant experiences.

Understanding Context

Diversity for its own sake has little meaning. Its value lies in the effect it may have on the ability to accomplish objectives, and that is a matter of context. Let's imagine, for example, that you hold a meeting attended by blacks, whites, Hispanics, and Asian Americans of both sexes. They differ in sexual orientation and physical abilities as well. They have various levels of education and have worked in many functional areas. Is this a diverse group? Yes, in terms of attributes. But does this group have significant diversity—similarities and differences that will bear on their ability to accomplish their objectives? We can't know until we know the context, the purpose of the meeting, and the mindsets of its participants.

Suppose the group is a collection of scientists who all believe passionately in a new scientific theory and have met to determine how to promote its acceptance. The most important quality here is a shared belief in the value of the theory, which makes demographic differences irrelevant. These people are likely to act in a very cohesive fashion with relatively little behavior diversity.

Now suppose the group are participants in a town meeting debating how to allocate an unexpected budget windfall. Here, attribute diversity is definitely significant because demographic differences may translate into highly divergent viewpoints.

Clarity on context is essential, especially for giraffes who hold managerial positions. Without this clarity, they cannot hope to work effectively with diversity.

Identifying Requirements

Giraffes, like elephants, must respond to the mixture of their own requirements and those of the head giraffe, the organization, and elephants. But before they can respond appropriately, they first must understand what those various requirements are.

Focusing on Self

This task is as complicated as it is critical. Giraffes, like elephants, can best start by identifying their own requirements. They must be able to distinguish among "nice to haves"—preferences, traditions, and conveniences—and bottom-line requirements. In doing so, they face a challenge not common to elephants. Because they have defined the norms in the past, they can be tempted to treat "nice to haves" as if they were requirements.

Jeff appears to have fallen into the trap. His religious beliefs frame his personal bottom line, and he advocates that the Bible's prescriptions about morality should do the same for his company. He treats his organization as an extension of himself.

Giraffes can avoid this trap by qualifying their key questions. For example, they can ask, "What are my bottom-line requirements, given the organization's purpose?"

Even giraffes who avoid this trap may fall into another and assign undue priority to their own requirements. The giraffe's goal is to contribute to the development of a house—even one owned by giraffes—that allows everyone to contribute fully for the collective good and to realize their expectations. Those who assign inappropriate importance to their own requirements hamper their ability to contribute to the building of such a house.

Giraffes, like elephants, sometimes neglect to take the time to explore their bottom-line needs. Young giraffes who identify strongly with giraffes are particularly prone to do so. Since giraffes dominate and define a situation, these young giraffes are tempted to say "me too" and adopt the "requirements" of their mentors and peers.

The difficulty is that giraffes differ greatly. Giraffes who count on others to tell them who they are and what they want can lose touch with their genuine identity and needs.

Focusing on Elephants

If giraffes are to create a house that engages everyone, they must identify the elephants' requirements. Three factors make this difficult.

First, because giraffes are so dominant, they can assume (without necessarily knowing it) that elephants are extensions of themselves. This makes it seem unnecessary to learn about the elephants' requirements and differences because, they assume, elephants will assimilate to their requirements. George appears to make this assumption. Although he advocates including those who are different, he assumes they will assimilate to the organization's way, and that his direct reports will conform to his way of doing things.

Second, a personal distaste for others' differences can prevent giraffes from learning the elephants' requirements as well. Several coaches disliked Dennis Rodman's behavior so much that they made no effort to understand and meet his requirements. They simply excluded him from their teams.

Finally, stereotypical thinking also blocks giraffes' ability to grasp the elephants' requirements. To know an individual's requirements, one must tap the essence of the person, not respond to caricatures or stereotypes. The more a giraffe thinks and speaks in stereotypes, the less likely he or she is to ferret out the elephant's requirements. George thinks in stereotypes. It will be hard for someone who says "minority" and thinks (consciously or unconsciously) "poor and undereducated" to understand the requirements of an affluent, upwardly mobile racial or ethnic minority.

Focusing on the Organization and the Head Giraffe

Just like elephants, giraffes find it hard to identify the boss's and the company's requirements, and for the same reasons: fallacious or outdated reasoning and assumptions, and poor communication on the part of managers. However, one complicating factor is unique to giraffes. Because they possess an affinity with the head giraffe and enjoy membership in the dominant insider group, they can see themselves as part of the organizational family and may take for granted that they understand its workings. They may also believe that their family membership entitles them to success. Giraffes who think in these ways see little need to gather data on the head giraffe's and organization's requirements.

Head giraffes harbor misconceptions as well. They may assume that giraffes are sufficiently connected to understand requirements and see little reason for extra effort on their part, so they neglect to communicate requirements directly and clearly. Head giraffes may also harbor another notion that works against communicating requirements. They may implicitly or explicitly communicate, "We'll take care of our own." As a result, they discourage "requirement" questions. They expect giraffes to do what they are told and to trust that they will be rewarded.

Paradoxically, giraffes in these settings can be less clear about business requirements than elephants, who know they must ferret these out for themselves. Such giraffes focus on staying in the family and reaping entitlement rewards. Their limited knowledge of business requirements keeps them poorly positioned to address diversity.

Lack of Trust

Giraffes who don't trust their head giraffes or organizations to create a house that engages all can see diversity as a zero-sum game. One group can be expected to win, the other to lose. To include diverse people and accept and use their differences is to increase the odds that giraffes will be excluded. Jeff and Kirk give voice to this fear. Jeff felt that he, a born-again Christian white male, no longer had a place in his company and decided to vote with his feet. Kirk believes that diversity will be good for his organization, but he feels that white men may pay a price.

One result of this distrust is that open dialogue disappears. Giraffes commonly share their concerns only among themselves. They do not talk with head giraffes or elephants, so they simply reinforce each other's views. No one has an opportunity to debate with them to make changes where they are needed.

Extraneous Agendas

Giraffes, like elephants, can have extraneous agendas. Jeff's religious agenda, while core to his identity, is extraneous to his organization's requirements. His wish to make the Bible's moral views the corporation's governing framework has pushed him toward outsider status.

Playing the Giraffe Card

White men who say, in effect, "I am a giraffe and I am being treated wrongly because of this," are mirroring elephants who play the elephant card. Both Kirk (Chapter 12) and Jeff (Chapter 11) play the giraffe card, but Kirk does it more frequently.

Does playing this card work? It might if the goal is to stop change and promote retreat in the direction of the previous status quo, especially if it rallies the giraffes into a public, unified position. Still, playing the giraffe card does have a downside, particularly in organizations committed to diversity progress. People may polarize, and members of the mix may retrench. Here, the use of the giraffe card is a minor or major disaster. It does not produce the desired results.

Whatever the public results, giraffes who play the giraffe card compromise their own ability to address diversity effectively. The dynamics set in motion by playing the giraffe card can slow their diversity management progress to a crawl.

Conceptual Confusion

Giraffes, especially if they are white males, can stumble over the fundamental diversity principles. All three of the white men interviewed see diversity as synonymous with inclusion, and by that they mean inclusion in terms of attributes (e.g., race, gender, sexual orientation). Only Kirk expresses openness to behavior diversity, and only Kirk is beginning to see white men and, by extension, himself as part of the diversity mix.

All three men want to do something for others who are "different"; each desires, in his own way, to do the right thing. Yet they all lack a framework for developing options. None of them recognizes the mixture of requirements, and only one of them fully endorses the business motive for diversity management. As a result, they've experienced frustration. Kirk attempts to teach himself through his diversity work and reading. George (Chapter 10) and Jeff are muddling through.

Failure to Appreciate Pioneering Role

Elephants venturing into giraffe country can easily see themselves as pioneers. Giraffes who receive these elephants are no less pioneers, but it is less obvious that this is so. As a result, they can continue to look to the past as a guide to future action. In truth they would be better served by girding themselves for a changing future.

Even building a house for a giraffe and an elephant is a pioneering task. Most homes—and organizations—are built for a relatively homogeneous group. Few are expected to work for a significantly diverse mix of occupants. Few giraffes have experience with this more challenging task. Yet their lack of awareness that they are pioneering hampers their attainment of diversity effectiveness. Because they don't understand diversity and their pioneering status, they don't appreciate the complexity and challenge of the situation. As a result, they don't realize that they need education, training, and development.

Strangely, even giraffes who know that they lack readiness do not transfer this understanding to head giraffes, who are expected to be all-knowing and take care of every situation. George, for example, acts as if his senior managers know what to do with and about diversity but simply refuse to do it, so he chastises them for lack of action rather than explore how he can assist in their growth. A major leap of faith and logic is not required to determine that head giraffes are as unprepared for diversity as giraffes.

Complicating matters further are those head giraffes who puff and posture as if they know what they are doing and cannot admit they are walking in the dark. Head giraffes who cannot say, "It's dark, and I could use a flashlight," attempt to pretend they are not pioneering.

The net effect is to hinder the creation and delivery of a theory, model, and tools that can help everyone: head giraffes, giraffes, and elephants. An inability or unwillingness to acknowledge the reality of pioneering hinders progress across the board.

Reliance on Elephants

In a similar way, giraffes can hide their own lack of readiness by relying on elephants to come up with diversity solutions. Often giraffes assume that because elephants are "diverse" they know all about diversity.

Typically what elephants can do well is tell giraffes what to do about *their* requirements, not about all the requirements in the mix. Giraffes who respond to those parochial recommendations do so with a growing awareness, and surprise, that elephants don't know everything about diversity effectiveness. This knowledge can become the giraffes' excuse for not pursuing diversity further—a prescription for a do-nothing disaster.

Dealing With "Isms"

Many would say that this factor should have led the list of challenges. Indeed, racism, sexism, and other isms hinder giraffes' ability to function as effective diversity respondents. However, this discussion of challenges indicates that giraffes unable or unwilling to move forward with diversity management may not be suffering from the isms. Any of the factors discussed here may be acting as hindering influences.

A significant implication is that any effort to remove hindrances to progress must have a diagnostic component to see which ones are operating.

FACILITATORS FOR MEETING THE CHALLENGES

Just as parallels exist between challenges facing giraffes and elephants, so do parallels between factors that can help them achieve diversity effectiveness.

Taking Charge

Giraffes are as prone to blaming their organizations for ineffective diversity management as elephants are. And they can be tempted to sit back and observe, to wait for the bosses to do something, or even to resist actively. Jeff, for example, monitored behaviors within his organization and resisted when he disapproved. George is content to do "what he can" within organizational constraints and criticize others for lack of action. Only Kirk, through his work with diversity councils and his reading, is moving into a leadership role.

Yet giraffes must accept leadership roles in their company's diversity efforts. To limit diversity concerns to individual behaviors is to stunt their company's ability to meet its viability requirements and diminish their own status as organizational leaders.

Accepting Pioneer Status

Giraffes will find it easier to assume leadership roles if they accept their status as pioneers. This helps them to see that the confusion and relative inefficiency that may characterize their efforts is due to the newness of diversity management and not their incompetence or prejudices.

Those who haven't distinguished between affirmative action and diversity management will find this hard to do. They know that affirmative action has been around for some time and think, "This isn't new." Giraffes like Kirk, who combine curiosity about diversity and comfort with the nuances of diversity management, can play a major role in contributing to the diversity maturity of their organizations.

Mentoring

Elephants report that mentoring around diversity issues is key to their organizational success, yet no giraffe reported asking for or receiving such mentoring. None appeared to think it was needed. They see themselves as outside the mix or don't realize they are pioneering. Yet pioneering giraffes, like elephants, need help. They can begin to get it by mentoring each other, then providing these services to others who want to address diversity effectively.

Those who mentor giraffes need not work for the same organization, and they need not always be giraffes. Elephants can help too. Multiple mentors with specialized roles can be especially helpful. The issues and feelings accompanying diversity are complex, and no one person has diversity management figured out.

Transferring Learnings

The diversity management process provides a structure for addressing all diversity mixtures. This broad applicability is important, for it allows people to begin developing skills by addressing mixtures that are compelling to them or relatively unstressful. It also allows them to examine previous experiences for lessons that can be applied to existing mixtures. Giraffes who can transfer learnings from one setting to another are likely to become effective diversity respondents.

Developing Mature Attitudes

Empathy

Empathy, the ability to put ourselves in another's shoes, can help giraffes understand and respond to diversity. This is particularly true when differences in one or more dimensions generate tension. We know that the capacity to carry on in the face of tension is an important aspect of diversity maturity. Giraffes whose personal experience includes elephant or outsider status in some realm are often more empathic than those without such experiences, and this background enables them to remain steadfast under stress or tension.

Kirk provides an example. He grew up in a single-parent home in a family that struggled economically; he was a minority in a mostly female department, and he has two sisters who are lesbians. These experiences enable him to view differences from an empathic perspective. His childhood experiences helped him to learn to focus on requirements. His work experience helped him to know how it feels to view oneself as "not the promotable choice." This combination of experiences prepared him to place his sisters' sexual orientation within a broader perspective. His requirement was to have a loving relationship with his sisters; his insight was the difficulty of being labeled an outsider.

Kirk's interview contains poignant glimpses into the perspectives of both giraffes and elephants. Should he choose to share his perspectives with members of each group, he could help them to understand each other better.

Tolerance for Ambiguity

Just as effective diversity respondents must learn to live through tension, they must also be comfortable with ambiguity. Diversity management calls for modifying the giraffe's house so that it works for both giraffes and elephants, and neither is disadvantaged. Since diversity management is new, no one knows exactly how the new house will be designed or how the group in the numerical minority will avoid minority status.

Giraffes know this. Even those who genuinely support diversity and diversity management can be ambivalent. They don't know if either is really in their best interests. Although Jeff and Kirk work in different organizations, they share a common concern. They're not entirely sure it is possible to build a house that works for giraffes and elephants both. This is not an unreasonable concern, particularly in situations where giraffes have reasons to doubt their management's diversity astuteness.

To become a diversity-mature giraffe is to accept ambiguity and become comfortable with the ambivalence that accompanies it. These ambiguities and uncertainties mean that the giraffe's decision to embrace diversity differs from that of the elephant. Elephants do so with hope and expectation. Giraffes do so with conviction and some trepidation about how matters will evolve. It is important to acknowledge this difference.

🦒 🦒 🦒

If giraffes are to become effective diversity respondents, they will have to work through some complex issues. They must, at a minimum, decide that diversity management is desirable for the organization and that the hard work of building diversity effectiveness will produce personal benefits for them as well.

Reaching that point of insight can be a stretch for people who have always believed they already understand how the world works and see no reason to change. A stretch of such fundamental proportion is definitely unsettling. The only reason to subject oneself to such discomfort is confidence that the long-run benefit is far greater.

PART FIVE
Moving Toward Diversity Effectiveness

14
The Individual Journey

It has become an axiom that diversity effectiveness in organizations requires the commitment of the head giraffe and changes in organizational culture and systems. And that's true. What's not true is that the head giraffe is the only person with diversity management responsibilities or that he or she can create a diversity-effective organization on his or her own.

The diversity effectiveness of any organization depends ultimately on a combination of factors: a committed head giraffe, necessary changes in culture and systems, and the willingness and ability of individual giraffe and elephant members to interact effectively with each other in the light of their different perspectives.

If an organization is honestly working toward creating an environment where genuine diversity thrives, it is because individual men and women, each in his or her own way, are making it happen. It matters not whether their motivation is wholly altruistic, or entirely for personal goals, or some combination. The end result is the same: as each person in an organization reaches new levels of diversity maturity and effectiveness, the organization overall and all of its members share in the benefits.

That's where you come in. In this chapter, we look at ways that you can take steps on your own toward becoming an effective diversity respondent.

ACKNOWLEDGE YOUR ROLE

You must begin by accepting responsibility for the state of diversity effectiveness in your organization. All else depends on this one courageous step.

Most people accept no responsibility for implementing diversity efforts. They think that's someone else's job. In one company I am familiar with, the CEO and his senior executives (the head giraffes) directed the midlevel managers to "take care of making changes." These managers, in turn, pointed to individual contributors and their union, saying they could do nothing in the face of such major hindrances. The individual contributors accused managers of failing to follow through, of not really caring. But no one pointed to himself or herself. Often the conversation doesn't even get that far. Instead, everyone shrugs and says, in effect, "It's all up to the boss," even though it may not always be clear which "boss" they mean.

In truth, all of these statements are partly right and partly wrong. All those "other" people and groups do have a role in achieving diversity effectiveness, just as do those attempting to deflect responsibility. Little progress will be made until the desire to make changes permeates the entire organization.

Why focus on your response to diversity when it may appear that others have the power? Because you're the only person you can control. Diversity management starts with you and spreads out to family, community members, and work colleagues.

EXAMINE YOUR ATTITUDES

One way to become clearer is to ask yourself the following questions:

"Do I see discussions about alternate ways of doing things as a waste of time?"

"Do I respond negatively when someone says, 'I think I have a better idea'?"

"Do I wince when others dress or groom themselves differently than I find attractive?"

"Does change make me uncomfortable?"

A yes answer to any of these questions indicates more comfort with inclusion than with diversity. It can alert you to the need to begin to see where you are cutting off opportunities for personal growth by excluding diversity before you have an opportunity to evaluate it objectively.

MONITOR YOUR BEHAVIOR

Often people who say they're eager to improve their diversity effectiveness don't stop to assess their own behaviors when confronted with diversity issues. They already "know" where others are and assume that they themselves are okay. But if you have accepted personal responsibility for diversity effectiveness and are ready to begin the journey, you must start by taking stock of how you customarily behave in situations where diversity creates tension.

One way to do this is to focus on seeing yourself in diversity-rich situations. A journal can help you do this. Such a journal, kept daily for at least two weeks, will provide you with a series of diversity snapshots that feature your diversity-related behavior. The point of the diary is to chronicle each encounter with diversity and your response to it. At the end of the period, review and analyze the entries by asking yourself the following questions:

- Did I capture all the diversity mixtures I encountered?
- What kind of tensions did I see?
- What kind of tensions did I personally experience?
- How comfortable was I with the tensions?
- What were my responses to the mixtures? To the tensions?
- How appropriate were my responses? Did they help to address requirements and issues or to make this more difficult?
- How flexible am I? Do I routinely rely on just one or two responses, or do I change my response to suit the situation?
- What is my layman's assessment of myself as a diversity respondent?
- Do I need improvement?

    🐘 What would be the benefits to me?
    🐘 How critical are these benefits?
    🐘 Am I willing to do the hard work of monitoring my be-
        haviors and changing those that don't contribute to di-
        versity effectiveness?

    You may want to record your observations in a slightly more formal structure. To do so, create a chart with places to record these factors:

    🐘 Location
    🐘 Situation
    🐘 Important differences and similarities
    🐘 Diveristy tension
    🐘 My response to this tension
    🐘 Outcome

    How might it work? Suppose, for example, that you attend a city council meeting where people discuss a local option sales tax to support construction of a new school. You would go home from the meeting and jot down as much as you could remember about what happened. But you would delay completing the chart. For that, you need some time for reflection. At the end of the week, return to your chart and complete the columns. Your entries might look something like the diversity management chart shown on the next page.

    Your personal records, whether in the form of a narrative diary or a more structured chart, should help you identify the diversity mixtures and tensions that you commonly encounter. They should also help you to see how you respond to diversity and these mixtures and tensions.

REVIEW YOUR PRIORITIES

At this point, pause and consider your own goals and priorities: your personal mission, vision, and objectives. Without this framework, no context for diversity decision making exists.

    Mission and vision relate to your overarching purpose in

My Diversity Management Chart

Location	Situation	Important Differences and Similarities	Diversity Tension	My Response to This Tension	Outcome
Town Hall	Discussion of local option sales tax	People with or without elementary-age children. Age Income	Those wanting and those opposing the tax Discussion became unpleasant	I suggested a time-out until council members create a document that details the benefits and disadvantages of both choices and convinced people to meet again in two weeks	People agreed after some hesitation; council members agreed to bring the information

life and a visualization of its achievement. Strategies describe plans for achieving mission and vision, while goals and objectives respectively reflect long- and short-term action priorities. Specifying these variables allows you to identify your personal compelling motives for wanting to strengthen your diversity abilities.

Compelling motives may or may not be work-related. Family, social, or religious settings may offer more priority challenges for many. You may, for example, want to respond more effectively to a neighbor with whom you have differences, or a son or daughter with whom there is tension. You may want to ensure that certain things get done in your community and need to work with diverse people to make this happen. It is important to begin where the compelling motives direct. Whatever you learn can be transferred later to other, lower-priority arenas.

GET READY TO LEARN

At this juncture, you should be motivated sufficiently to do what is needed to build your conceptual understanding of diversity. Recognize that acquiring a working understanding of these concepts will take time and effort.

Start adding to your store of knowledge. Read books and articles, attend seminars, use self-instruction vehicles, and then practice using the concepts as you learn them.

Many people find it helpful and also enjoyable to enlist a learning partner. You can discuss your readings with each other and swap seminar notes. It is especially valuable to have someone to talk to about your diversity journal. You can help each other analyze the encounters you recorded and make sure neither of you misses any significant dynamics. Talking candidly with your learning partner about the feelings that these encounters provoked can be illuminating.

Teaching offers another opportunity to get clear on basic concepts. The person doing the teaching often learns more than the students. Corporations increasingly are asking managers to teach the diversity concepts.

DESIGN A PLAN

If, as you reflect and learn, you discover perspectives, ideas, and behaviors that can keep you from reaching the level of diversity maturity you desire, think through what you could do to work on those areas. Review your diversity journal for clues to the dynamics that you find troubling. Talk it over with your learning partner, if you have one. Then sketch out a plan of how you will go about this journey of personal growth.

Suppose, for example, that you discovered a pronounced tendency to act on personal preferences instead of requirements. An action plan here would focus on strengthening your ability to identify decision points, sort out relevant requirements from traditions, preferences, and conveniences, and debate the pros and cons of alternatives. This plan calls for slowing the decision-making process, in hopes of gaining insights on how you can become more comfortable relying on requirements as decision-making criteria.

This in turn might generate additional developmental plans. Let's assume, for example, that you realize after analyzing your decisions that you rely on personal preference because of poor communication skills. When there is a communication exchange about something you have a preference on, you tend to see the exchange as an opportunity to make your case rather than a chance to explore perceptions and learn. You might decide to focus on listening and exploring views in hopes that after a while, your preference tendency will become less strong.

PRACTICE WHEREVER YOU CAN

We often hear a protest that goes something like this: "I'd like to increase my own diversity effectiveness, but my company just doesn't care." Indeed it is true that sometimes a person of great determination who is trying to make changes is stymied by the environment within which he or she functions.

If you find yourself in such an environment, you can still begin your journey toward diversity effectiveness without waiting for your company to catch up. How? By practicing diversity

skills in other settings: within your family, church, neighborhood, or community groups.

In fact, many people who are introduced to diversity concepts immediately see applications to nonwork settings. One
manager said, "I know a lot of churches that need this." Another
observed, "I usually have to struggle to see an application of
work practices to my family situation. In this instance, I had to
struggle not to think of my family in so many applications."

People who begin the journey in outside settings can bring
their knowledge and skills into their corporation when the tim-
ing is appropriate. In doing so, they can assist their company's
journey to diversity effectiveness.

The journey is not an easy one. Becoming an effective diversity respondent takes commitment, effort, and time. About now
you may be asking, "Is it worth it?" We believe it is. The ability
to move skillfully among people and situations that differ from
those we are accustomed to is a gift far beyond the specific benefits it confers. It expands our world and gives us the confidence
to dream big and accomplish much.

🦒 15 🐘

A House for Diversity

Organizations, like individuals, vary greatly in the degree to which they address diversity effectively. For them, the task is to create what I have called a "managing diversity" environment. Within the context of the giraffe and elephant fable, the task would be for the giraffe to create a house for diversity—that is, to share in the responsibility of achieving a fit between the elephant and the house while maintaining a house that worked for him and his family as well.

Head giraffes in organizations can begin this process by publicly stating their belief that the presence of employees who are effective diversity respondents will foster the organization's progress. They must also support and reward employees who pursue diversity maturity and skills. They must provide senior and middle managers responsible for nurturing a managing diversity environment with the tools and support they need as well.

REQUIREMENTS FOR A MANAGING DIVERSITY ENVIRONMENT

A managing diversity environment requires two things: a collective diversity maturity on the part of managers and an organizational culture that supports these managers in addressing diversity effectively. This two-part breakdown is similar to that I used to describe an effective diversity respondent. But there is one major difference: The core diversity skills defined as essential to the effective diversity respondent give individuals a very specific framework with which to address individual situations. Organizational culture is quite different. This culture, which comprises the company's guiding assumptions and the systems and practices that emanate from them, acts as an envelope within which all other activities take place. Its impact is overarching.

Few organizations have solved all of their culture issues. Diversity-mature ones are busy addressing them. Managers in these organizations are asking questions such as:

> "We have a culture of being one big happy family. Sounds good on the surface, but we now know this makes it difficult for us to manage diversity effectively. It keeps us from engaging all employees, and it unfairly entitles traditional workers. But we're afraid of the consequences of eliminating this idea. How can we keep the cohesiveness we need while letting go of the 'family' notion?"

> "We know that the special status of the marketing department creates discord with the other units. But this status has a practical basis. It is marketing that generates our profits. How can we confer equal status on the other units without disrupting our profit-making potential?"

Because I have written elsewhere about the culture change process, this chapter focuses on organizational diversity maturity. It is essential to remember, however, that diversity efforts often succeed or fail based on the impact of the organization's culture.

ORGANIZATIONAL DIVERSITY MATURITY

When discussing an organization's diversity maturity, we are concerned with many of the characteristics that determine individual diversity maturity. But we're looking at managers on a collective basis.

We want to know, for example, how clear managers as a group are around mission and vision, the degree to which they have formulated a compelling business motive for addressing diversity effectively, and the extent to which they understand diversity concepts. We also want to know how, as a group, they make diversity-related decisions regarding inclusion and exclusion and whether they habitually place differences in context when responding to them. We're interested in whether they are willing and able to cope with the complexity and tensions that a diverse workforce brings as well. Finally, we want to know if they have developed a clear framework and process that identifies which organizational diversity efforts will be initiated and in what order, and if they have developed a strategic plan that incorporates this process. The chart on pages 220 and 221 outlines the behaviors of organizations that have attained different levels of diversity maturity as they relate to these characteristics.

You are probably not surprised that the specific qualities and attitudes of organizations echo a list we might create for individuals. However, the organizational mandates have a broader base of application.

WHY IT MATTERS

An organization's diversity maturity will do much to determine how easy or difficult it will be for individual contributors to become effective diversity respondents. Responses to diversity aren't made in a vacuum. They take place within communities, families, companies, and work teams. Even the most effective diversity respondents will have only limited impact if their organization does not back them up.

Diversity-mature individuals in a diversity-immature environment will have difficulty honing their skills. When that happens, organizations lose in many ways. Individual workers become cynical. Their managers, seeing no benefit to pursuing maturity, put their energies elsewhere. Thoughtful employees

may decide to leave. As a result, the organization loses its competitive advantage.

By the same token, effective diversity respondents working
in a supportive environment produce skilled organizations. A
principle of reciprocity is at work here: Individuals need a supportive, diversity-mature organization; the organization needs
the behaviors and insights of diversity-mature individuals. One
set of dynamics reinforces the other.

Let's look at how those characteristics that demonstrate diversity maturity play out in organizations.

CHARACTERISTICS OF DIVERSITY MATURITY IN ORGANIZATIONS

Mission and Vision

Leaders in diversity-mature companies develop and communicate two missions and visions: a comprehensive mission and vision, and a diversity management mission and vision. The first
serves as the glue that holds different and disparate people and
organizations together. The second provides motivation for cor-
poratewide efforts to build diversity effectiveness.

These leaders begin this process by examining their comprehensive vision and mission and identifying the diversity mixtures that are explicit and implicit in them. The mixtures they
identify become the raw data from which to create the diversity
mission and vision. They then link the missions and visions together at every opportunity. This communicates to individual
contributors as well as managers the essential message: "We're
embarked on a diversity management effort because we can't
meet our business objectives and requirements without it."

In contrast, managers in low diversity-mature organizations
may be clear about the organization's mission and vision. However, they don't connect diversity management with these or
with the organization's continued survival. They make no reference to diversity when articulating the company's mission and
vision. And they make no reference to vision and mission when
making diversity decisions. Instead, they act as diversity fire-

fighters, responding to crises and seeking to resolve them as soon as possible.

In moderate diversity-mature organizations, managers have connected diversity management adeptness with achieving mission and vision. But this connection has not been formalized through development of a diversity management mission and vision.

A Compelling Business Motive

Leaders in high diversity-mature companies do more than link their mission and vision to diversity effectiveness. They know that they must have a business motive for managing diversity, and this motive must be compelling. They develop and articulate such a motive by identifying those diversity mixtures that are strategic——those that must be addressed successfully if they are to remain viable. They know that the most significant diversity mixes may be workplace mixtures, not workforce mixtures. They may, for example, find that addressing mixtures created by acquisitions and mergers or functional diversity may reap the most benefits.

They address whatever diversity issue has the most potential to contribute to viability and profit. They then transfer the learnings from these efforts to workforce diversity issues.

Awareness of a compelling business motive makes diversity management relevant and worthwhile. It drives people and organizations through the tension and complexity of the process in search of competitive advantage. Lack of this awareness hinders.

Leaders in low diversity-mature organizations see no business motive for addressing diversity, which they define essentially as race and gender. To these leaders, addressing diversity is a cost, not a benefit.

Leaders in moderate diversity-mature organizations want to find a compelling business motive and often work hard to develop one, but they lack the flexibility to consider workplace mixtures as significant. As a result, they may create a motive based on a workforce mixture that may be important but lacks the impact on the bottom line that is needed to make the business motive compelling.

Clarity About Diversity Concepts

Managers in diversity-mature organizations define diversity appropriately, understand the difference between inclusion and diversity, and know the differences between the diversity approaches. They act in ways that are congruent with their understandings.

Managers in moderate diversity-mature organizations may have knowledge about the nature of diversity and its dynamics and about the differences among the diversity approaches, but they are inconsistent in putting this knowledge into action.

Managers in low diversity-mature organizations lack conceptual clarity and have made no link between diversity management and the viability of their organization. To them, diversity is limited to making things right with minorities and women. To the extent that managers consider conceptual and process frameworks, they are confused. To them diversity and affirmative action are one. Both exist solely for the benefit of minorities and women.

Inclusion and Exclusion of Attribute and Behavioral Diversity

One area in which an organization's diversity maturity becomes quickly apparent is in its managers' response to attribute and behavior diversity. Diversity-mature organizations have one standard by which to make decisions about inclusion and exclusion around this diversity: What effect will including this individual who demonstrates these characteristics have on our ability to meet organizational objectives? They respond accordingly.

Organizations that demonstrate low diversity maturity respond in one of two ways. Some organizations have little openness to any diversity. They operate within the law but go no further. In these organizations, managers lean informally toward exclusiveness without necessarily discussing or questioning their leanings. As a result, minorities and women employed at the company complain of being tokens. In such organizations, behavior diversity is excluded when possible, tol-

erated when not. Organizations showing these extremes of responses are becoming relatively rare.

Organizations demonstrating equally low diversity maturity
may fit a second, seemingly different, profile. Managers in these
organizations readily accept attribute diversity but discourage
behavior diversity. Those who are "different" are expected to
assimilate to organizational norms around requirements and
nonrequirements.

Two types of very different companies are likely to fit this
profile. The first might be a large manufacturing concern with
no consumer products and little "diversity" history. Its managers look around, see the diversity activity, and wonder briefly if
they are missing something. They see no business benefit and
feel no compelling motive. Still, they worry that they should do
something about "it," whatever "it" might be. They briefly
explore the issue, then conclude, "The benefits [whatever they
might be] aren't worth investing much time or money on."

The second might be a large corporation with awards for
its pioneering "diversity" work in recruiting, promoting, and
retaining minorities and women. This company, often cited na-
tionally as a "good place" for minorities and women, sports a
wide variety of "diversity" activities and a comprehensive "diversity" plan. However, those inside the organization know that
all isn't as it appears to be. The organization does, in fact, welcome attribute diversity, but around behavior diversity, it insists
on assimilation. Its leaders have not changed their culture, systems, and practices in response to a diverse workforce. Instead,
they focus on outreach to women and minority communities,
special developmental thrusts to prepare members of these
groups for promotions, and activities designed to convey that
"diversity" is valued. Such activities are appropriate in many
settings, but they barely touch the surface of the diversity arena.
To call a thing "diversity" is not to make it so.

Moderate diversity-mature organizations have still another
challenge. Managers in these organizations know that they must
address both attribute and behavior diversity. But doing so has
proven to be a stretch. These managers, many of whom initially
embraced attribute diversity, are finding their enthusiasm wan-
ing. They were unprepared for the behavior diversity that came

with attribute diversity and lack the skills with which to respond. Many, however, are catching their second breath. They're reading books, taking courses, and otherwise preparing themselves to meet the challenge.

Focus on Requirements

Diversity-mature organizations delineate and stress requirements. About these they are firm. They design their policies, systems, and processes to meet these requirements, and they refuse to let preferences, conveniences, and traditions intervene.

Organizational leaders at one company demonstrate such maturity. These leaders were under pressure because of the company's fuzzy promotion policies at the upper management levels. They decided to do something about it. They began by implementing policies and systems that ensured that all qualified comers—insiders and outsiders—would know about and be able to apply for position openings. Then they developed a process for determining each position's genuine requirements.

They implemented the system with trepidation. The selection of upper-level positions in the past had leaned heavily on preferences. Senior managers with the most influence put forth their best mentorees, and these people tended to be hired.

The first several months under the new system were, in fact, painful. A year into the process, two outsiders and one insider had been chosen. And two things had become clear: (1) The three individuals who had been hired were exceptionally capable and qualified for the positions they had filled, and (2) these three had introduced considerable diversity around nonrequirements.

Leaders noted that the company's environment wasn't working as well for those hired externally as for the insiders, and so they made another decision. They are currently updating organizational systems and practices to accommodate behavior as well as attribute diversity. Without such changes, these highly capable individuals could find the company inhospitable and rigid, and perhaps decide to seek their fortunes elsewhere.

Managers in moderate diversity-mature organizations often understand that only requirements should dictate assimilation, yet they demand acculturation around nonrequirements as well. They may allow others to express differences they find distasteful and then fret about having to do so. These managers, however, often know what they don't know. And they begin to seek process grounding as well as skill improvements.

Managers in low-diversity-mature companies often have not linked the notion of diversity and requirements. They either discount the notion of diversity to the extent that this is possible, or link attribute diversity so closely with affirmative action–type efforts that they fail to consider diversity within the context of requirements. Acceptance of attribute diversity is often seen as "something we have to do."

Interestingly, very successful companies frequently have the greatest difficulty with this notion of requirements. They think that they possess the formula for success, and that all that is needed is to do more of the same. After a number of successful years, they see their organizations as institutions and take their viability for granted. They mix requirements, traditions, personal preferences, and conveniences in justifying their actions.

As long as the organization's environment stays stable, this intertwining of motives serves the organization well. It is when the environment shifts that they have problems. They must identify and adopt new requirements. But the old ones, so intermingled with preferences, traditions, and conveniences, resist giving way. The tenacity of these old requirements can confuse companies and their leaders, locking them in a time warp. This makes it difficult to respond to the environment as it is rather than as it used to be.

The requirements issue often comes to the forefront as companies go global. One manager stood in front of his colleagues and vigorously proclaimed that the company would not compromise its values and standards as it went global. Later, several managers went to him and asked questions about instances abroad where challenges existed. Unprepared to discuss diversity and its implications, the manager simply smiled.

A diversity-mature manager in a diversity-mature company would instead have reaffirmed a commitment to requirements but not necessarily to home office preferences. He or she would

Levels of Organization Diversity Maturity

Variable	Low Maturity (1)	Low Maturity (2)	Moderate Maturity	High Maturity
Mission and vision clarity*	Low-high	Low-high	Moderate	High
Understanding of compelling business motive*	Low	Low-moderate	Moderate	High
Concept and process clarity*	Low	Low	Low-moderate	High
Inclusion/exclusion of attribute diversity*	Tokenism	Very accepting	Conflicted acceptance	Very accepting
Inclusion/exclusion of behavior diversity*	Low acceptance	Low acceptance	Conflicted acceptance	Very accepting

Focus on requirements	Include/exclude all regardless of impact on meeting organizational objectives.	Assimilation around requirements, traditions, preferences, and conveniences.	Acculturation around requirements and some nonrequirements.	Assimilation only around requirements.
Comfort with diversity tension*	Low	Low	Moderate	High
Development of framework process	No recognition that one is needed.	No recognition that one is needed.	Managers understand the need but have not developed a process.	Managers have developed and are adhering to a process.
Strategic diversity management plan	Managers have no plan, or use one designed to facilitate only inclusion.	Managers have no plan, or use one designed to facilitate only inclusion.	Managers are in the process of developing a plan.	Managers have a plan and are using it to guide implementation of the process.

*Refers to managers collectively

have known that these might prove inappropriate in another culture.

Companies that become adept at focusing on requirements routinely place both attribute and behavioral differences in context when deciding how to respond to them. They have communicated to all employees the idea that differences are acceptable as long as they do not get in the way of achieving objectives. An enormously successful retail company based in a major city provides an example.

The company, known for the crispness of its associates' dress and manner and its intolerance of untidiness, expanded into a rural area known for its informality and laid-back lifestyle. When the new store was not as successful as expected, the company took stock and in the process looked at its customers.

What its leaders found is that these rural customers, unlike their urban counterparts, preferred an informal atmosphere that said, "Come as you are." They complained that the slickness of the new store made them feel they had to dress up before going shopping. The company caught the message. Sales associates became less brisk; the company's preference for regimentation was shelved. Business picked up.

Companies with less diversity maturity often separate "diversity" from requirements. Their managers lack any consistent way in which to structure their response to differences. As a result, these responses often display considerable variation and unevenness.

Comfort With Diversity Tension and Complexity

Managers in diversity-mature organizations acknowledge that life is more complex when diversity is expressed, but they understand that this is part and parcel of diversity dynamics. They are willing to experience the tensions that can arise when significantly different people work together.

This tension can be experienced at any scale. It may be present in the interactions between two departments located in a single building, or between two subsidiaries in widely separated countries. The organization's response is the same: tolerate the tension while taking the time to analyze the circumstances fully.

Then, undaunted by the presence of complexity, the leaders are in a position to take effective action. They may decide, for example, that the tension among two work teams is contributing to greater productivity and leave it alone. Alternately, they may decide that tension among members of a cross-functional team is preventing the team from achieving its goals and take swift action.

Because managers in diversity-mature organizations understand the link between diversity management and organizational success, they experience no undue stress in response to the diversity tensions.

Managers in moderate diversity-mature organizations may focus on achieving harmony, thus stifling creativity and innovation as well as tension. Those in low diversity-mature organizations may simply stifle diversity, thus suppressing or denying the presence of tension.

A Clear Framework and Process

Diversity-mature companies adopt a framework and process to guide them in their diversity efforts. These keep them on track by identifying what will be required for success and how success will be measured.

Companies with less diversity maturity lack such a framework and process. These companies often fall into diversity traps—for example:

- *Activity trap*. Managers measure success in terms of the number and magnitude of activities.
- *Public relations trap*. Managers measure success by how well the media and other external entities speak of their efforts.
- *Training trap*. Managers measure success by the amount of training that has been completed.
- *Event trap*. Managers measure success in terms of events such as companywide diversity conferences.
- *Awareness trap*. Managers measure success by the degree of "awareness" that exists.

None of these approaches is wrong, and each may be appropriate at a given juncture and place. Without a guiding framework and process, however, they can give organizations and their managers a false sense of diversity progress.

A Strategic Plan

Diversity-mature organizations acknowledge a need for continued progress in diversity management and make plans to take action. One common approach is to develop a strategic plan for diversity management. The organization's leaders develop this plan early and adhere to it steadfastly, thus keeping their organization on track with its diversity efforts. This strategic diversity management plan serves several purposes.

- To inform all organizational participants of the organization's purpose and direction in implementing diversity management efforts
- To motivate organizational members to meet their diversity management goals
- To provide the structure, clarity, and accountability that allow them to do so

To ensure that the plan does this, organizational leaders must, at a minimum, do the following:

- Develop a compelling business motive in three key areas: the workforce, workplace, and marketplace. Without this motive, efforts are seen as extraneous, and commitment is minimal.
- Identify the diversity-related issues that must be addressed. It is essential that they define diversity broadly enough that it has strategic significance.
- Delineate the order in which the tasks must be addressed. Some initiatives will be simultaneous; others, by necessity, must follow each other.

Next, leaders must plan how and when they will address the issues. They must delineate which approaches will be needed, what strategies will be used, who will be responsible for their success, and when detailed planning and implementation will take place.

Organizational leaders in moderately diversity-mature organizations may have a "diversity" plan; however, it is unlikely to be considered strategic, although the plan may well include plans for diversity management as well as affirmative action efforts. These leaders have simply not yet put the necessary diversity understandings and concepts together into a cohesive whole. There is evidence, however, that they intend to do so.

Organizational leaders in low diversity-mature organizations see little reason for a strategic diversity management plan. They either have an affirmative action–type plan or see diversity issues as too insignificant to warrant strategic planning. These organizations can become defendants in diversity-based lawsuits.

IN CONCLUSION

Do business organizations really need to attend to diversity issues? Only if they intend to stay in business. Any company that believes it can ignore diversity concerns and still thrive in the modern global environment—which is diverse by definition—is set on a disastrous course.

The stumbling block for many organizations is some continuing confusion about exactly what diversity is. This is a holdover from earlier days, when many people thought "diversity" meant bringing in workers from minority groups. Often motivated by morals or personal ethics, at other times responding to legal realities, they wanted to include those who had historically been denied opportunities.

A focus on inclusion is not wrong from a social or legal standpoint, but it's very ineffective from an organizational one. The problem is that no matter what the original intentions, inclusion inevitably produces diversity with all of its complexity and tensions. Most organizations seeking representation didn't expect to get diversity too. They assumed that nontraditional

workers would leave their differences at the door. It quickly became clear, however, that they would not do so.

Organizations have been coming to grips with this reality
ever since it became clear. In truth, few, if any, organizations
have reached full diversity maturity. Currently moderate diversity-mature corporations operate at the forefront of the diversity
field. They are today's diversity pioneers. Some are advancing
step by step, while others appear to be going in circles. Most
pioneers are just beginning to grasp the need for a systematic,
guiding process.

Managers in these organizations know that their effectiveness in addressing diversity-related issues will affect their organization's business viability. But still they struggle.

They are likely to continue to struggle. Diversity is too complex and multifaceted to be managed easily. Organizations and
managers that persist, however, will be amply rewarded.

The rewards of effective diversity management are recipro-
cal. Diversity-mature organizations achieve competitive advantage by enhancing productivity and nurturing the development
of employees at all organizational levels who respond to differences and similarities in focused and effective ways. These
individuals, by their presence and actions, bring a diversity
management capability to the organization. Together, these individuals and their organization build a house for diversity—one
where diverse people are maximally productive and flexible in
pursuit of organizational and individual objectives.

Appendixes

Appendixes

Appendix A
Action Options

In *Redefining Diversity*, I identified eight action options, ways that people and organizations typically respond to diversity:

1. *Increase/decrease.* This refers to a decision to increase or decrease the amount of diversity by including or excluding components and the variability among them. Seminars designed to "expand the breadth of thinking" of senior executives are attempting to increase diversity of thought. Excluding people who fail to meet certain expectations in behavior or performance is an attempt to decrease diversity.

2. *Deny.* This is a decision, often unconscious, to minimize diversity by explaining it away. When someone says, "I don't understand why the departments are fighting; we all work for the same company," that is an attempt to avoid the reality of diversity. So are apparently benign comments such as "People are really the same under the skin."

3. *Assimilate.* This involves minimizing diversity by insisting that "minority" components conform to the norms of the dominant factor. A requirement that employees speak English only is an attempt to enforce assimilation; so is a decision from corporate headquarters that all divisions, regardless of how different or similar they might be, must use the same systems.

4. *Suppress.* This means minimizing diversity by removing it from consciousness. The individual knows of a difference but deliberately pushes it from his or her awareness.

A familiar example is "Don't ask; don't tell," the U.S. military's policy on sexual orientation. So is the directive that many organizations give to their employees not to discuss political or religious affiliations at work.

5. *Isolate.* This is a decision to address diversity by including mixture components that are different but setting them aside—for example, putting the R&D function in a different location or locating the medical records department in the basement of a medical complex. Holding workplace social events during a time when second-shift employees cannot attend is isolation as well. People can be isolated physically or as a consequence of inadequate information.

6. *Tolerate.* This option, a very common one, addresses diversity by fostering a room-for-all attitude but limiting interactions among mixture components to superficial exchanges. A statement such as "Those folks in the other building are crazy, but I guess we have to work with them" illustrates the dynamics of toleration. Often those who tolerate feel magnanimous; those who are tolerated feel demeaned.

7. *Build relationships.* This option strives to address diversity by encouraging an attitude of acceptance and understanding. Sensitivity training to help participants let go of their prejudices and stereotypes is an example of this approach; so are cross-functional social events designed to help workers get to know each other.

8. *Foster mutual adaptation.* This option is based on a solid understanding of requirements. When the circumstances involve genuine requirements, the action required is mutual adaptation: All parties make whatever adjustments are needed to satisfy the requirements and get the job done. When the circumstances involve nonrequirements, differences are simply accepted as fact. Managers using this option expect people and organizational units to adapt and change where requirements are involved but to accept differences elsewhere.

These action choices can be and usually are used in combination.

None of these is inherently good or bad in itself; it all depends on the context. Finally, each option can be used with any diversity mixture.

Of the eight options, only the last, foster mutual adaptation, unequivocally endorses diversity. This doesn't mean that foster mutual adaptation is the only valid option. Effective diversity respondents aren't focused on maximizing diversity. Considering the breadth of diversity that exists today in the population from which American organizations draw their workers, it's quite likely that will take care of itself! Instead, organizations aim to address diversity in ways that foster the achievement of individual and organizational objectives. In all likelihood this will require the use of all of the options.

Appendix B

Pre-Test–Post-Test Score Sheet

PDMI Pre-Test			Level of Diversity Maturity	PDMI Post-Test		
Question	Response	Score		Question	Response	Score
1			High Diversity Maturity (85–100) You demonstrate substantial diversity maturity when dealing with the differences and similarities that people bring to the workplace.	1		
2				2		
3				3		
4			Moderate Diversity Maturity (70–85) You have thought about diversity, and are open to learning new ideas and behaviors for addressing it. You have demonstrated a desire to address diversity more effectively but are unclear as to how to go about it.	4		
5				5		
6				6		
7				7		
8			Low Diversity Maturity (50–70) You have not thought much about differences and similarities in the workplace or about how these can be addressed in the most productive way. You still have a long way to go toward becoming as effective as you can in addressing diversity.	8		
9				9		
10				10		
Total Score				Total Score		

Appendix C
PDMI Pre-Test
Answer Key

I have identified five key characteristics of diversity-mature individuals. Your score on the PDMI is based on the extent to which your answers reflect these characteristics. Score your answers first. Then turn to Appendix D and reexamine your answers on the basis of these characteristics.

1. **a.** *5 points.* Although you are trying to air differences, other options for this scenario demonstrate a more active management of differences.

   b. *5 points.* This is a "do-nothing" response.

   c. *10 points.* By looking at what's good for business, you'll have a clearer understanding of how to proceed.

   d. *7 points.* This kind of engagement has the potential for beneficial effects.

2. **a.** *5 points.* You are reacting to diversity (or the lack of it) rather than taking an active role.

   b. *10 points.* You're actively soliciting opinions from others and exposing yourself to some potentially challenging discussions.

   c. *7 points.* This may improve the situation, and it shows your awareness of the need to manage diversity. However, to become a more diversity-mature manager, you may want to go beyond recruitment to engagement.

    d. *5 points.* You are, in essence, saying, "This is not my problem."

3. **a.** *7 points.* Your intentions are good.

   b. *10 points.* The diversity-mature manager recognizes that diversity is good for business.

   c. *5 points.* If you adhere to this way of thinking, you'll have difficulty internalizing the benefits of diversity management.

   d. *5 points.* You may be looking out for yourself but not for your company.

4. **a.** *5 points.* This approach may be efficient, but it does not acknowledge anything unique about your customer base.

   b. *5 points.* Unless you are particularly astute and experienced, you should call on others to provide help and make sure your proposal is on target.

   c. *10 points.* This shows you can tolerate tension in the interest of getting a superior product.

   d. *7 points.* You show sensitivity to the local community but you also need to be aware of doing what's good for business.

5 **a.** *7 points.* You're managing diversity with the complainers.

   b. *5 points.* Your lack of action signals discomfort with the tension that managing the situation more directly might provoke.

   c. *10 points.* You are opening a discussion with a staff member to manage diversity in the workplace.

   d. *5 points.* This is issuing a directive. While important, it is a relatively passive action. It doesn't demonstrate the more direct involvement that managing diversity would entail.

6. **a.** *10 points.* If your coworker is meeting requirements, her style in doing so is of no concern.

   b. *5 points.* You are asking your supervisor to intervene on the basis of your preferences, not requirements.

   c. 5 points. You are assuming that to be different from you is to be deficient. Your coworker is meeting requirements and has given no signs that she wants help.

   d. *7 points.* You are directly asking your teammate for her opinion. If you see your invitation as just that and are willing to take no for an answer, you are giving yourself and others an opportunity to hear what your teammate has to say.

7. a. *5 points.* You are declining to get involved in a potentially difficult situation.

   b. *5 points.* You are validating one set of concerns but not another set.

   c. *7 points.* You are establishing a means for dispute resolution.

   d. *10 points.* You are focused on what is best for your company.

8. a. *7 points.* You're acknowledging that there may be factors that could be addressed to help this individual improve relations with the customer.

   b. *5 points.* Although you're probably interested in satisfying your customer's needs, you aren't supporting your own staff.

   c. *5 points.* You're demonstrating your commitment to meeting customer needs, but you're ignoring your staff member's abilities and devaluing her worth.

   d. *10 points.* You're basing your decision on requirements.

9 a. *5 points.* A group meeting with a strong common interest may demonstrate less diversity even though its members differ greatly in attributes.

   b. *7 points.* You're demonstrating your understanding that when discussing diversity, beliefs and behaviors are more significant than attributes.

   c. *5 points.* This group demonstrates demographic differences, but it may not be very diverse.

   d. *10 points.* You're demonstrating that you understand that the concept of diversity is complex and that each situation must be evaluated in context.

10. **a.** *10 points.* The diversity-mature individual recognizes that good employees may not always come in stereotypes.

b. *7 points.* This may seem like a win-win situation, but it indicates that you're not willing to model acceptance of diversity in situations where this diversity will not affect the ability to meet requirements.

c. *5 points.* You are not taking responsibility for your staff or your customers.

d. *5 points.* Although you may be placating your customer (temporarily), you are not addressing the matter.

Appendix D

Characteristics of the Diversity-Mature Individual

1. Accepts diversity management responsibility.

2. Possesses contextual clarity.
   —Knows himself or herself.
   —Knows his or her organization.
   —Understands key diversity concepts and definitions.

3. Is requirements-driven.
   —Differentiates among preferences, traditions, conveniences, and requirements.
   —Places differences in context when making include/exclude decisions.

4. Is comfortable with diversity tension.

5. Engages in continual learning.

Appendix E

Interpreting Your Scores on the Pre-Test PDMI

No matter what your score on this Personal Diversity Maturity Index, this book can help you to boost the confidence and wisdom with which you address diversity.

Your scores on the pre-test can help you to gauge the judgment and clarity with which you respond to diversity and its inevitable complexities. As such, it can give you valuable information about your effectiveness in addressing the differences and similarities that play out as you and your workplace associates work together to achieve personal and organizational goals.

I have identified three levels of diversity maturity: high diversity maturity, moderate diversity maturity, and low diversity maturity. Following the explanations of each of these levels are some suggestions for reading the book in ways that might maximize your learning. I believe, for example, that each reader will benefit from working with a learning partner—someone with whom to talk over the ideas and share perceptions. I also believe that the more challenging you find the concepts, the more likely you are to benefit from discussing them with others.

These are, of course, only suggestions. Read the book in the way that works best for you.

85–100: High Diversity Maturity

Congratulations. Your answers suggest that you demonstrate substantial diversity maturity when dealing with the differences and similarities that people bring to the workplace. Each individual's level of diversity maturity, however, is contextual. Typically, no one is equally mature in all settings.

To benefit most from *Building a House for Diversity*, I suggest that you approach the book in the following ways:

◁ *Learn to identify the characteristics that make you a mature diversity respondent.* This will give you the confidence that operating out of a framework and process provides and that intuitive behaviors may not give you. Appendix D summarizes the characteristics of diversity-mature individuals. The readings and analyses flesh them out.

Expand the numbers and types of situations where you behave in diversity-mature ways. Suppose, for example, that you readily accept differences in style and behavior on the part of coworkers but feel challenged and irritated when your child or other family member behaves in ways you wouldn't choose. In this case, you might want to read the book with two goals: to enhance your already impressive workplace diversity maturity and to explore how you can transfer the book's teachings to your family setting. (Chapter 12 provides an example of an individual who has been able to do this.)

◀ *Learn the core diversity management skills that allow you routinely to address specific diversity situations in the most effective way.* (It is the combination of diversity maturity and mastery of the core skills that will allow you to become an effective diversity respondent.)

◁ *Work toward becoming a diversity management champion.* Give some thought to setting up a group for the purpose of reading the book and sharing your responses and perspectives with others.

70–85: Moderate Diversity Maturity

Your answers suggest that you have thought about diversity and are open to learning new ideas and behaviors for addressing it. You are likely to have demonstrated a desire to address diversity more effectively, but you are unclear as to how to go about it. In fact, you may be ideally positioned to benefit from the book. You should be able to grasp the key concepts quickly and enhance your diversity maturity level with relative speed.

To benefit most from this book, you might want to:

1. First read Chapters 1 and 2 of the book, referring to Appendix D as needed.
2. Then move on to read the book in its entirety.
3. Reread Chapters 1 and 2 to "lock in" the basic concepts.
4. Reread the stories and analyses, comparing and contrasting them. The idea is to understand more clearly how the roles that we are assigned influence our perceptions and perspectives. This review will help you understand yourself and others.
5. Make notes of your observations, and look for opportunities to discuss the book and your observations with others.

50–70: Low Diversity Maturity

Your answers suggest that you may not have thought much about differences and similarities in the workplace or about how these can be addressed in the most productive way. Many of the book's ideas may be new to you or may challenge your firmly held beliefs. I urge you to persevere. Achieving diversity maturity can help you to advance your own career and make your organization as productive and successful as it can be. It can help you to improve the quality of your personal relationships as well.

To get the most benefit from this book, you might want to:

1. Select a learning partner.
2. Read Chapters 1 and 2 carefully, referring to Appendix D as needed.
3. Identify the ideas that you find challenging or confusing and discuss these with a learning partner.
4. Read these chapters again.
5. Turn to the part that focuses on the role that you typically play in your organization (head giraffe, elephant, giraffe)

and read the stories and analyses found there. Identify the individuals who respond to diversity in ways that are both most like you *and* most unlike you. Read the analyses of these individuals with particular care. Ask your learning partner to do the same and to discuss his or her response with you.

6. Complete your reading of the book, discussing your general reactions with your learning partner.

7. Reread the various parts, comparing and contrasting the stories and analyses. The idea is to understand more clearly how the roles that we are assigned influence our perceptions and perspectives. Doing so will do much to help you understand both yourself and others. It may also suggest places and ways where you will benefit from changing perspectives or behaviors.

8. Continue to discuss your observations and responses with your learning partner.

Appendix F
PDMI Post-Test

Now that you've read the book, it's time to complete the post-test PDMI. Then you can compare your pre- and post-test scores to see the extent to which your diversity maturity has evolved as a result of reading the book.

This Index, like the pre-test PDMI, is scenario-based. Read each of the ten individual scenarios and review the possible responses to each situation. Then write the letter of the response that most closely reflects how you would respond to that scenario on the score sheet provided in Appendix B. When you have completed the post-test PDMI, turn to the post-test answer key in Appendix G for the scores applied to each response. Record your individual and aggregate scores on your score sheet. Then turn to Appendix H for the interpretation of your aggregate score and for suggested next steps.

1. *You and another midlevel manager have been asked to prepare an important report for your company's board of directors. After extensive planning, organizing, and analysis, you and your colleague begin to write the report. It soon becomes evident that your colleague, whose primary language is not English, has weak writing skills. Although he holds an advanced degree from a prestigious university, he is unable to write clearly and accurately. What would you do?*

   a. Realize that to prepare a high-quality report, you will have to work long hours to make up for his shortcomings. You're annoyed, but you do it.

   b. You like your colleague, and you realize that somewhere along the way he did not receive the kind of instruction and education that would enable him to write well. You shoulder the responsibility for preparing the report.

c. Figure that your colleague must have skills that the company values—after all, he is the midlevel manager selected for this assignment. You talk over the situation with him and determine where he can best contribute to the report.

d. Get mad. Tell your supervisor that your colleague is not pulling his weight and you need someone else to step in and fulfill his responsibilities.

2. *You are a human resources director of a department store. A group of employees comes to you to complain about other employees who speak Spanish when on breaks, when stocking shelves, and even at times to customers who are looking for specific items. The complaining employees report that they have noticed the Spanish-speaking employees laughing when non-Spanish speakers walk by. The employees who have come to you are uncomfortable with the situation and want you to do something about it. Which of the following describes what you would do?*

a. Call a meeting or distribute a memo that clearly explains to employees that only English is to be spoken during working hours.

b. Explain to the complaining employees that they should work it out with the Spanish speakers on their own and that the store has no problem with employees' speaking Spanish in the store.

c. Talk with some of the Spanish-speaking employees and ask them to try not to speak Spanish when there are non-Spanish speakers around.

d. Facilitate a dialogue between the offended employees and the Spanish speakers to see if there are any situations where English must be spoken if you are to meet requirements (for example, where physical safety is involved). Work toward an agreement that with the exception of these situations, Spanish may be spoken. Help members of the two groups explore their mutual distrust and find ways to resolve it.

3. *You work in a manufacturing plant. One of the staff members you supervise is a single mother with two young children. She has always received good reviews. She asks you for help in arranging flextime so that she can spend more time with her children. However, your company does not have a policy regarding flextime. How would you respond?*

    a. Suggest that the two of you work together to form a proposal to present to the company's decision makers.

    b. Tell her that you understand her situation but that matters are out of your hands because the company hasn't chosen to adopt flextime.

    c. Suggest that she take the matter to your company's employee grievance committee. Let her know that you'll support the request if it makes it through that group.

    d. Work with her to do an analysis of her job and others like it to determine how working during their preferred times will affect the ability of her and others to get their jobs done. Base your response to her dilemma on the results of the analysis.

4. Of the following, which most accurately describes your approach to diversity in the workplace?

    a. I try to make sure that my company hires people of different races, ethnicities, and backgrounds.

    b. I consciously seek out opportunities to work with people of different races, ethnicities, and backgrounds.

    c. I act as a facilitator between employees when I see situations of cross-cultural misunderstandings.

    d. I don't necessarily enjoy being around all of the people I work with, but I accept differences that annoy me so long as they don't affect my ability to do my job. I draw the line when a difference makes it impossible for me to get my work done.

5. *You are in charge of a group that is preparing a major sales call to a large company. One of your strongest colleagues is openly homosexual, and you are concerned that his behavior and mannerisms could adversely affect your prospects of gaining this company's business. What would you do?*

   a. Talk with the employee, explain your concerns, and ask him to tone it down a bit for the sales call.

   b. Reassign his duties so that he does behind-the-scenes work and someone else goes in his place to call on the potential customer.

   c. Nothing. There is no concrete evidence that this person will not continue to perform well.

   d. Nothing. You value your colleague's contributions and company and see no reason to chance hurting his feelings.

6. *You work for a somewhat straitlaced company that has recently acquired a successful high-tech business whose staff members are used to setting their own hours, wearing jeans and T-shirts to work, and ordering out for pizza when the mood hits. You have been given the responsibility for helping to integrate the new business into your company. Which of the following would be your response?*

   a. Call a meeting of your company's leaders and tell them to "get with the program" because the high-tech business is imperative if your company is to be successful.

   b. Call a meeting of the staff from the newly acquired company. Explain to them that although your company values their creativity and work, it has an image to uphold, and they must conform to the company's policies and procedures.

   c. As your staff and the new staff begin to interact, look for and talk about their similarities and encourage them to notice the positive things about each other.

Point out ways in which they might learn to work together.

    d. Set up a task force with representatives from both groups to develop policies and procedures that will allow the company to meet its acquisition objectives.

7. *You notice that your office is experiencing a lot of turnover among women and that employee morale is low among those remaining. You are a senior manager. What would you do?*

    a. Raise the issue at a managers' meeting. Before deciding what to do, see if others have made the same observation.

    b. Go to your human resources department and explain your concerns. Ask it to review turnover patterns.

    c. Quietly meet with some staff who have left and others who are dissatisfied. Listen to their concerns, and see if there is a pattern to the causes of discontent.

    d. Ride it out. Your office has gone through swings of this sort before and will survive. Also, it's not part of your job description to worry about those sorts of things.

8. *You are the president of a midsize company, and one of your long-term vice presidents has retired. You need to fill that slot and have two candidates in mind, both current employees. Both have excellent performance records and get along well with the staff. One is a member of a racial minority group, and the other is white. Your company does not have a minority vice president, and you are under considerable pressure from stakeholders to promote a minority to a senior management position. How do you decide which one to promote?*

    a. Choose the minority candidate. You will demonstrate your commitment to affirmative action and diversity, thus satisfying stakeholders and alleviating the pressure that is being put on your company.

    b. Consult with other senior managers to see if the culture is ready for a minority vice president. Go with their recommendations.

     c. Create two vice-presidential slots and promote both individuals.

     d. Open the search process to include others outside the company so that when you eventually choose one candidate, you can't be accused of bias in your decision.

9. *You are an investment banker, and your firm has a subsidiary in an eastern European country. The staff in that overseas office is overwhelmingly white and male, but your firm is committed to diversity in the workforce. What do you do?*

     a. Wait until you have identified a problem within the subsidiary that requires talent from your organization to solve. Then select a group of your most talented employees, regardless of race, ethnicity, or gender, to work within the subsidiary and resolve the problem. As part of the debriefing of the experience, point out the value that the diversity of the team provided.

     b. Do nothing. The overseas office is performing well, and tending to business is more important than making a social statement.

     c. Say nothing. You have no control over who chooses to apply for jobs. Besides, that's the way the overseas office has always looked.

     d. Review the office's performance and emerging markets. Is the current composition best for your company's profitability? If it is, leave it alone. If not, develop a local recruitment campaign to increase the number of minority and female employees.

10. *As division head of your company's manufacturing operation, you attend a managers' meeting where affirmative action and diversity are discussed. The managers complain that they are unable to identify qualified minorities and women to promote. You observe that they are almost all white men. It's clear that minorities and women have a difficult time achieving success and recognition in your company. How do you respond to this information?*

a. Form a committee of your staff to determine why the division lacks minorities and women at higher levels.

b. Change promotion practices to encourage greater upward mobility for minorities and women.

c. Acknowledge the lack of diversity at upper levels and document how this can and is having a negative impact on the business.

d. Institute affirmative action measures because you are afraid that if the situation goes on much longer, your company will be sued.

Appendix G
Post-Test Answer Key

Your score on the post-test PDMI is based on the extent to which your answers reflect the five key characteristics of diversity-mature individuals. After scoring your answers, you may want to return to Appendix D and reexamine your choices based on these characteristics.

1. **a.** *7 points.* Your reaction is understandable.
   b. *5 points.* Although your response is probably motivated by compassion, you run the risk of tolerating diversity at the expense of what's good for business.
   c. *10 points.* You respect your company's decision about what's good for business.
   d. *5 points.* Your reaction is understandable, but you need to focus some energy on solving the problem.

2. **a.** *5 points.* Your response does not respect diversity, does not allow for meeting customer needs, and does not guarantee freedom to communicate openly on the part of Spanish speakers.
   b. *7 points.* Although you are helping the complaining employees to understand diversity, you are not demonstrating an ability to listen seriously to their complaints.
   c. *5 points.* This response may minimize the contributions of Spanish speakers and does not respect diversity.
   d. *10 points.* You show a willingness to seek a solution that focuses on the requirements for the job, not personal preferences or grievances.

3. **a.** *7 points.* You are demonstrating that you take the employee's problem seriously and will invest in helping to achieve a mutually beneficial outcome. However, you have not addressed requirements.

   b. *5 points.* You are saying that this is not your problem to manage.

   c. *5 points.* You are saying that this is not your problem to manage. Promising to stand by her once she has taken action does not demonstrate maturity.

   d. *10 points.* You are taking the time to analyze the effect of her request on the ability to meet organizational requirements while demonstrating your willingness to entertain her request seriously.

4. **a.** *5 points.* You are trying to change the makeup of your company.

   b. *7 points.* By seeking out opportunities, you are demonstrating your willingness to take chances and grow personally. This is a first step in taking responsibility for personal and organizational change.

   c. *5 points.* This is a reactive stance.

   d. *10 points.* You are basing your reaction to differences on the effect that the difference has on your ability to do your job.

5. **a.** *5 points.* You are having what might be a difficult conversation with your colleague, but you're assuming a lot.

   b. *5 points.* If he's that strong a colleague, why assign him to behind-the-scenes work?

   c. *10 points.* The best predictor of a colleague's future performance is his past performance. To assume that your colleague won't do well is to insert your own biases or assumptions into the situation.

   d. *7 points.* He's included, but for the wrong reasons. At work, what's at issue is the individual's ability to do the job. You're shortchanging your colleague and your company by including him to be "nice."

6. **a.** *5 points.* At the same time that you're welcoming the new company's standards, you're devaluing the ones that your own company's staff has adhered to.

  b. *5 points.* Although you've opened discussions with staff members in the newly acquired company, you're telling them how to dress and behave, which may stifle the creative spirit that produced their business success.

  c. *7 points.* It's a start, but these folks will need to work well together long before they feel comfortable with each other.

  d. *10 points.* The only thing that will allow these two groups to work effectively together is a commitment to a common goal and an agreement on how to go about achieving it.

7. **a.** *10 points.* It's hard to bring up the tough questions, but your willingness to do so shows commitment to the company and its employees. Your willingness to test your own observations before jumping to conclusions is praiseworthy too.

  b. *5 points.* Although you may be following standard business procedure, you're passing the buck to a certain extent, rather than investing your time and energy.

  c. *7 points.* You are gathering information from the most relevant sources. But without checking out your assumptions with others first, you may be jumping the gun.

  d. *5 points.* You have observed a problem but are remaining silent.

8. **a.** *10 points.* At this time, it clearly is a requirement that your company demonstrate its commitment to promoting minorities. To fail to do so is to signal indifference to stakeholders.

  b. *7 points.* The willingness to include others in the decision is admirable. But organizational culture is strong, and senior managers are likely to resist going against past practices. Change occurs when one person or group steps out and does what is needed, not when people wait until making a move feels comfortable.

c. *5 points.* This is a weak way out that will probably cause greater upheaval than resolution.

d. *5 points.* Bad idea. Besides, this is not about proving a point. It's about doing what is best for the company, given its current priorities.

9. **a.** *7 points.* Trying to transfer your company's commitment to workforce diversity is a worthy goal. But you're unlikely to achieve it by trying to make the point before the two companies have developed common objectives and some sort of working relationship.

   b. *5 points.* Passive response.

   c. *5 points.* Passive response.

   d. *10 points.* You're basing your response on what is best for the business.

10. **a.** *5 points.* This is a minimal response.

    b. *7 points.* It's a good idea, and you'll no doubt want to do it after you're sure you have the facts. But to do it now would be acting without adequate understanding.

    c. *10 points.* If you do this in a timely fashion and communicate the results to your senior management, you will be setting the stage for a committed response on their part. You will have established a compelling business motive for action.

    d. *5 points.* You should have done this already.

Interpreting Your Scores on the Post-Test PDMI

Your score on the post-test PDMI can help you to assess your overall diversity maturity and the extent to which you have taken in the concepts in the book and made them your own. A comparison of your pre- and post-test scores can also help you to see how your diversity maturity has evolved as a result of reading the book.

The scoring remains the same as that in the PDMI pre-test. A score of 85 to 100 indicates high diversity maturity. One of 70 to 85 indicates moderate diversity maturity. A score of 70 or

lower suggests that you may still have a way to go toward becoming as effective as you can in addressing diversity.

Although your PDMI scores can give you valuable clues as
to the likelihood that you will respond effectively to differences
and similarities in the workplace, they do not tell the whole
story.

They can, for example, assess the extent to which you recognize diversity maturity but not the extent to which you demonstrate it. And they are not intended to assess your core diversity
management skills.

Regardless of your scores on the post-test PDMI, practice
and continual learning will be needed if you are to grow in your
diversity maturity and further enhance your diversity effectiveness.

Key to practicing in a way that allows for ongoing improvement is a method for recording and monitoring your diversity-
related interactions. The Diversity Management Chart that appears in Chapter 14 can provide such a method. Make several
copies of the sheet, found in Appendix H. Insert these sheets
into your personal planner so that you can reach them easily
and record on them often. Use your sheets daily until you see
patterns emerge and effective action become natural. Then refer
to them periodically to update your memory and monitor your
ongoing progress.

Ongoing learning requires access to information sources
that allow you to update your knowledge and revitalize your
interest. One source of such information is our web site, *www.
rthomasconsulting.com.* We invite you to visit us there.

Finally, we suggest that you talk to those around you about
diversity-related issues. Make use of your insights and practice
your skills in as many arenas as possible. Teach others, take
risks, and make note of the benefits to yourself and your organization of your enhanced ability.

Appendix H

Diversity Management Journal Chart

My Diversity Management Chart

Location
Situation
Important Differences/Similarities
Diversity Tension
My Response to Diversity Tension
Outcome

R. Thomas Consulting & Training   ''We understand diversity. We wrote the book.''

Notes

Index

distaste for, 191
enhancing success of people with, 133
factors determining, 66–67
integrating, 57–58
in management style, 96–97
racial, 96
sophistication about, 62
understanding, 6
different perspectives, 6–7
disappointments, 156–157
discrimination, 85–86
disillusionment, 105–106
diverse workers, integration of, 57–58
diversity
ambiguity about, 178–181, 183–184
business motive for, 14–15, 60
challenges of, 35
clarity about, 15–17, 34–35
See also conceptual diversity
diversity awareness, 62
barriers to, 49
diversity effectiveness
challenges for leaders in, 53–63
for insiders, 188–199
for outsiders, 140–150
practicing, 209–210
diversity learning, 119–121
diversity management, 6
accepting role in, 203–204
chart for, 207
in Chicago Bulls, 32–34
factors in success of, 47–52
intuitive understanding of, 51–52
journal chart for, 255–257
leaders' responsibilities in, 62–63
as plant manager, 45–46
rewards of, 226
diversity manager
making of, 37–52
natural, 25–36
personal background of, 47
working with teams, 47–48
diversity maturity, 76–78, 88–89, 99–102, 111–112, 122–123, 134–136, 160–162, 171–173, 182–185

characteristics of, 214–225, 238
importance of, 213–214
model for, 62–63
organizational, 212–213, 214–225
diversity mixture, 176–177
ability to analyze, 20–21, 78, 89, 102–103, 113–114, 124, 137, 162–163, 174, 186
ability to identify, 20, 102, 113, 136–137, 162, 173–174, 185–186
ability to recognize, 78, 89, 124
in Chicago Bulls, 32–33
definition of, 5
different components of, 6–7
emotion-laden, 61
making work, 57–58
recognition of by insiders, 188–189
of stakeholders, 58
diversity role models, 164
diversity skills, 11
core, 20–21, 78–79, 89–90, 102–104, 113–115, 124–126, 136–138, 162–163, 173–174, 185–186
testing of, 121–122
diversity tension, 7, 18, 74–75
ability to analyze, 20–21, 78, 89, 102–103, 113–114, 124, 137, 162–163, 174, 186
ability to identify, 20
comfort with, 78, 101–102, 112–113, 123, 185, 222–223, 238
coping with, 12, 17–18, 88
sources of, 96–97
on team, 121–122
tolerance of, 32
diversity traps, 223
diversity-mature individuals, 11–17
dominant component members, 8

education, 66
effective diversity respondent, 10–19
African American man as, 111–115
African American woman as, 99–104
Asian American woman as, 86–90

Printed in the USA
CPSIA information can be obtained
at www.ICGtesting.com
LVHW031447040824
787161LV00010B/69

9 781400 232413